D1061333

UNFINISHED BUSINESS

Unfinished Business

. . .

RACIAL EQUALITY IN AMERICAN HISTORY

Michael J. Klarman

OXFORD
UNIVERSITY PRESS

2007

OXFORD

UNIVERSITY PRESS

Oxford University Press, Inc., publishes works that further
Oxford University's objective of excellence
in research, scholarship, and education.

Oxford   New York
Auckland   Cape Town   Dar es Salaam   Hong Kong   Karachi
Kuala Lumpur   Madrid   Melbourne   Mexico City   Nairobi
New Delhi   Shanghai   Taipei   Toronto

With offices in
Argentina   Austria   Brazil   Chile   Czech Republic   France   Greece
Guatemala   Hungary   Italy   Japan   Poland   Portugal   Singapore
South Korea   Switzerland   Thailand   Turkey   Ukraine   Vietnam

Published by Oxford University Press, Inc.
198 Madison Avenue, New York, New York 10016
www.oup.com

Library of Congress Cataloging-in-Publication Data
Klarman, Michael J.
Unfinished business : racial equality
in American history / Michael J. Klarman.
p. cm.— (Inalienable rights series; bk. 2)
Includes bibliographical references and index.
ISBN 978-0-19-530428-2
1. United States—Race relations.
2. Equality—United States—History.
3. African Americans—Civil rights—History.
I. Title.
E185.K545 2007
305.896'073—dc22
2007011369

1 3 5 7 9 8 6 4 2
Printed in the United States of America
on acid-free paper

To Lisa

Contents

. . .

CONTENTS

CONTENTS

Illustrations

. . .

Editor's Note

. . .

We hold these truths to be self-evident, that all men are created equal, that they are endowed by their Creator with certain unalienable Rights....

—THE DECLARATION OF INDEPENDENCE

. . .

No American should be unfamiliar with the history of race in the United States. America's struggle to come to terms with the continuing dilemma of race has posed the most fundamental challenge in our effort to define ourselves as a nation. In *Unfinished Business: Racial Equality in American History,* the third volume in this series on Inalienable Rights, Michael Klarman offers an insightful, frank, and provocative analysis of this most difficult issue.

Klarman traces the story of race in America from the very beginning into the twenty-first century. Although we like to imagine that the history of American race relations is one of slow but inevitable progress, Klarman demonstrates that progress has been "episodic, not ineluctable." Moreover, although we like to think otherwise, Klarman maintains that Americans have rarely reformed race relations simply because it was the right thing to do. Rather, racial progress has often been an unintended consequence of other events, such as wars, population migrations, and economic forces. We also like to believe that law has played a profound role in promoting racial progress, but Klarman suggests that courts have often supported racist institutions, retarded progress, and reflected rather than shaped progressive racial mores.

The events that make up this history are often surprising, sometimes moving, and occasionally mortifying. Before the American Revolution, slavery was common throughout the colonies. Slaves were generally viewed as mere property. They could be mortgaged and seized by creditors to satisfy a debt. At the time of the Revolution, 10 percent of the residents of New York were slaves.

Although the Declaration of Independence proclaimed that "all men are created equal," most of those who signed the Declaration did not believe this sentiment included blacks, and the United States Constitution plainly recognized the right of states to preserve the institution of slavery.

As Klarman shows, over the next half-century free blacks in the North enjoyed only limited rights and lived in constant fear of kidnapping and enslavement. Indeed, the Supreme Court ruled in 1842 that northern states could not constitutionally impede in any way the right of slave owners to recapture fugitive slaves. States like Illinois, Indiana, and Iowa banned black migration, and even in the northern states abolitionists were harassed and physically assaulted. In 1857 in the *Dred Scott* decision, the Supreme Court ruled that because the framers of the Constitution had regarded blacks as "beings of an inferior order" who possessed "no rights which the white man was bound to respect," even free blacks could not qualify as citizens for purposes of the federal Constitution.

Klarman's history then takes us through the Civil War, the Emancipation Proclamation, the enactment of the Thirteenth, Fourteenth, and Fifteenth Amendments, the era of Reconstruction, and the collapse of black rights in the South. The late nineteenth century saw the rise of the Ku Klux Klan, the emergence of the Black Codes and racial segregation, rampant lynching, and the Supreme Court's decision in *Plessy v. Ferguson*, endorsing the principle of "separate but equal."

Klarman contends that it was World War II and America's fight against fascism that provided the primary impetus for racial change in the mid-twentieth century. But despite the triumphs of *Brown v. Board of Education*, the civil rights movement, the Civil Rights Act of 1964, and the Voting Rights Act of 1965, progress over the past fifty years has been fitful, at best. Although the United States has moved beyond slavery, lynching, poll taxes, and state-imposed segregation, many racial barriers remain.

As Klarman notes, racial segregation in housing and education have increased dramatically since *Brown*, the unemployment rate for blacks is roughly twice that for whites, the average black family has only about 10 percent of the wealth of the average white family, and more black men are in prison than are attending college. Although blacks comprise less than 12 percent of the population, they are more than 50 percent of the prison inmates. Moreover, an increasingly conservative Supreme Court has placed serious constitutional obstacles in the path of further racial reform. As a consequence, Klarman concludes that "for many blacks, the goals of equality and racial integration are as distant today as they have ever been." By highlighting America's uneven progress toward a more racially just society, Klarman sheds important light on why racial inequality persists and, even more frustratingly, why it has increased in recent years.

April 2007   Geoffrey R. Stone

Acknowledgments

. . .

I AM GRATEFUL to several students at the University of Virginia School of Law for their research assistance: Lincoln Bisbee, Brooks Hickman, Charlie LaPlante, Josephine Liu, Ray McKenzie, Kelly Phipps, Richard Rothblatt, and Stephanie Shuler. Two students, Katherine Twomey and Corinne Lane, not only helped with the research but also read the entire manuscript, offering many helpful suggestions. I am also grateful to Sarah Carr for help with illustrations and Laura Bower for secretarial assistance. The reference librarians at the law school ("Refdesk," as they are fondly known) were, as always, enormously helpful with tracking down sources, confirming facts, and generally making my life easier.

Several friends and colleagues read the manuscript and offered incisive suggestions for improvement: Liz Magill, Jim Ryan, Reuel Schiller, and Chris Schmidt. I am especially grateful to Michelle Morris, who not only read the entire manuscript and provided detailed comments, but also helped research a good deal of it and illustrated it pretty much by herself.

Dean John Jeffries was, as always, enormously supportive of my work. I am also grateful to Geof Stone and to Dedi Felman, who invited me to participate in the Inalienable Rights series, encouraged me to write more quickly and concisely than I am wont to do, and offered many helpful comments and suggestions along the way.

Charlottesville, Virginia   Michael Klarman
                                             March 2007

UNFINISHED BUSINESS

Introduction

. . .

ON SEPTEMBER 15, 1963, Ku Klux Klansmen in Birmingham, Alabama, dynamited the Sixteenth Street Baptist Church, killing four black schoolgirls. Within hours of the bombing, two other black teenagers were killed in Birmingham, one by white hoodlums and the other by the police. It was the largest death toll of the civil rights era.

In his inaugural address earlier that year, the governor of Alabama, George C. Wallace, had declared, "In the name of the greatest people that have ever trod this earth, I draw the line in the dust and toss the gauntlet before the feet of tyranny and I say segregation now, segregation tomorrow, segregation forever." In June Wallace fulfilled his campaign pledge to stand in the schoolhouse door, physically blocking the entrance to the University of Alabama before, in a carefully planned charade, stepping aside in the face of superior federal force.

Later that summer, Wallace encouraged extremist groups to resist school desegregation, which federal judges had ordered in

The Sixteenth Street Baptist Church in Birmingham after it was bombed on Sept. 15, 1963

several Alabama cities for the fall. In Birmingham mobs of angry white citizens took the governor at his word, bombing the home of a black lawyer who was involved in school desegregation litigation and causing a minor race riot. Wallace defended the rioters, whom he insisted are "not thugs—they are good working people who get mad when they see something like this happen."

Threatened with contempt citations by federal district judges, and overmatched by President John F. Kennedy's federalization of the state national guard, Wallace relented, protesting that "I can't fight federal bayonets with my bare hands." The schools desegregated, but within days, the Sixteenth Street Church had been bombed. Wallace received much of the blame. Martin

Luther King Jr. accused the governor of "creat[ing] the climate that made it possible for someone to plant that bomb," and President Kennedy, noting "a deep sense of outrage and grief," thought it "regrettable that public disparagement of law and order has encouraged violence which has fallen on the innocent."

Repulsed by the murder of schoolchildren, tens of thousands of Americans attended memorial services and protest marches. Some expressed their grief in letters to the National Association for the Advancement of Colored People (NAACP). A white lawyer from Los Angeles explained, "Today I am joining the NAACP; partly, I think, as a kind of apology for being caucasian, and for not being in Birmingham to lend my physical support." A white youngster from New Rochelle wrote: "How shall I start? Perhaps to say that I am white, sorry, ashamed, and guilty.... Those who have said that all whites who, through hatred, intolerance, or just inaction are guilty are right."

A black veteran of World War I from South Carolina, who had "seen many things that have been irksome" in his seventy years, including the lynchings of blacks and the murder of civil rights leaders, told the NAACP that "nothing in my life has had the effect upon me [that] the bombing of the Church and the Murder of the six Negroes in Birmingham [had]." He prayed that God would not "let these children die in vain."

The NAACP urged its members to "flood Congress with letters in support of necessary civil rights legislation to curb such outrages." The association's executive secretary, Roy Wilkins, demanded that the federal government "cut off every nickel" going to Alabama. Reflecting the outrage of their constituents, northern congressional representatives demanded that the administration's pending civil rights bill be strengthened.

As southern white resistance to progressive racial change turned increasingly violent, northerners began to demand intervention by the federal government to end Jim Crow. The Supreme Court's decision in *Brown v. Board of Education* (1954) had helped foment that violence by crystallizing southern white resistance to racial change, radicalizing southern politics, and bolstering the political careers of racial extremists such as Wallace.

At first glance the history of American race relations appears to be one of slow but inevitable progress. In the seventeenth century, blacks in Africa were enslaved and brought to the American colonies. In the late eighteenth century, the institution of slavery was fatally wounded in the North by the Revolutionary War. In the mid-nineteenth century, it was abolished altogether by the Civil War. White southerners replaced slavery with a system of racial subordination known as Jim Crow—a system that began to deteriorate by the middle of the twentieth century. In 1954 the Supreme Court declared it unconstitutional, and the civil rights movement of the 1960s finally destroyed it. Today blacks sit on the Supreme Court and in Congress, and some of the nation's leading cultural icons are black: Oprah Winfrey, Bill Cosby, Michael Jordan, and Tiger Woods. The last two secretaries of state have been African American, and a black man, Barack Obama, appears to be a viable presidential candidate for 2008.

Appearances can be deceiving, however; the true story of American race relations is much more complicated. Progress has been episodic, not ineluctable. The Revolutionary War put slavery on the defensive in the South, but it then grew more deeply entrenched. Southern blacks won the right to vote during Reconstruction, but then had it taken away. It was harder for blacks in the South to vote or attend an integrated graduate school immediately after *Brown* than before.

What has caused the ebb and flow of race relations in American history? On one view Americans have become more racially egalitarian when forced to confront the tension between the national creed of universal equality and practices of racial discrimination.

This view is naive: Americans have rarely reformed racially oppressive practices simply because it was the right thing to do. Before the Civil War, northern whites sought to constrain the spread of slavery primarily as a means of preserving the federal territories as a white enclave. In 1948 President Harry S. Truman desegregated the federal military largely because he needed black votes to win reelection. The federal government urged the Supreme Court to condemn racial segregation in *Brown* principally in order to deprive the Soviet Union of a powerful propaganda weapon during the cold war.

Rarely has racial progress been achieved without strong pressure from African Americans. In 1941, when confronted with a threatened march on Washington by one hundred thousand blacks, President Franklin D. Roosevelt issued an executive order barring race discrimination in defense contracting. In the 1960s massive street protests by southern blacks, which provoked brutal white retaliation, ultimately forced the national government to enact landmark civil rights legislation.

Yet pressure from blacks alone has rarely been sufficient to induce whites to do the right thing; supportive political and social conditions have proved essential to progressive racial change. Wars, internal migrations, shifting political coalitions, and technological advances have played vital roles in American racial reform.

Racial progress has often been an unintended consequence of other developments. The Civil War was not initially fought to end slavery, and the goal of World War II was not to launch a civil rights movement; yet such were the consequences of these wars. The justices who decided *Brown* cannot have imagined that their decision, by radicalizing southern politics and encouraging violence against peaceful demonstrators, would eventually pave the way for federal civil rights legislation.

Regional variation has been a driving force in the history of American race relations. Had the North not ended slavery before the South did, there would have been no Civil War. Had northern whites not begun to reject white supremacy by the 1950s, no southern civil rights movement would have been possible.

Yet in the North, too, the history of race relations has been one of ebb and flow. Blacks lost the right to vote in many northern states during the Jacksonian era, and northern blacks were more likely to be segregated in public accommodations and schools in 1920 than they had been in 1890.

No matter how shabby their treatment, though, northern blacks could vote (at least after the Fifteenth Amendment was ratified in 1870), and they could organize in protest; southern blacks could do neither. Northern blacks used these rights, in part, to challenge the oppressive treatment of southern blacks. Before the Civil War, free blacks in the North were leaders in the abolitionist movement and the Underground Railroad. In the twentieth century, northern blacks lobbied the federal government to legislate against lynchings and to curtail the disfranchisement of southern blacks. Had northern racial mores not been relatively tolerant, southern Jim Crow would have been far more impervious to change.

Furthermore, southern whites were so anxious about potential northern challenges to white supremacy that they often acted in ways that, paradoxically, undermined their cause. Southerners pushed so aggressively for federal government guarantees regarding slavery that they ultimately convinced many northerners that a slave power conspiracy threatened their liberties. The violent resistance of southern whites to *Brown* so appalled northern television audiences that they demanded federal government intervention to suppress Jim Crow.

The history of race in America is partly one of law. Law established slavery and white supremacy; law also ended those practices. To what extent did law shape racial mores, and to what extent did it simply reflect them?

Southern states enacted laws to segregate blacks and to disfranchise them, but many of these measures seem to have been mostly symbolic. Most southern railroads segregated blacks before laws were enacted to require them to do so. Most southern blacks had been disfranchised through force and fraud before poll taxes and literacy tests were adopted to formally restrict their political participation.

Conversely, laws that contravened entrenched racial mores were often disregarded. In the late nineteenth century, laws barring discrimination against blacks in hotels and restaurants were systematically ignored. An 1875 federal statute prohibited racial discrimination in jury selection, yet after 1910, no blacks sat on southern juries for decades. Perhaps not only was law generally unnecessary to secure white supremacy, it was also insufficient to suppress it.

Legislatures produce one sort of law, courts another. How much have judicial rulings influenced the course of racial equality in American history?

Whether the Supreme Court has, on balance, been more of a friend or a foe to racial minorities is a surprisingly close question. To be sure, *Brown*, which invalidated state-mandated racial segregation in public schools, was an enormous victory for racial equality. Yet before the Civil War, the Court regularly interpreted the Constitution to protect the interests of southern slaveholders. During and after Reconstruction, the Court invalidated civil rights legislation. And more recently, the justices have invalidated affirmative action plans and legislative schemes designed to enhance minority political representation.

Even progressive racial rulings, such as *Brown*, have reflected societal mores more than they have shaped them. In the late 1890s, when most of the nation supported white supremacy, the Court rejected constitutional challenges to racial segregation and black disfranchisement. By the time the justices had become more racially progressive, so had much of the nation. The ruling in *Brown* reflected the antifascist ideology of World War II, the contributions of black soldiers to the war effort, the growing political power of northern blacks, and the cold war imperative for racial change.

Racial minorities can only benefit from civil rights rulings to the extent they are enforced, which many of them have not been. In 1917 the Court invalidated laws requiring the racial segregation of neighborhoods, but residential segregation grew worse, not better. *Brown* was almost completely nullified in the South for an entire decade. Other progressive race rulings have been more effective. In 1944 the Court barred the exclusion of blacks from Democratic Party primaries, and black voter registration in the South increased dramatically. Political and social conditions influence the efficacy of civil rights rulings.

Court decisions can also matter in less direct ways: raising the salience of issues, educating opinion, and motivating supporters and opponents. Indeed, litigation itself, whether or not successful in court, can have similar educational and motivational effects.

How much have conditions for racial minorities improved over the course of American history? How linear has the progression toward greater racial equality been? What conditions have enabled progress? How much has the law mattered, and how much have Court decisions mattered?

It is to these questions that we now turn.

CHAPTER ONE

. . .

The Founding

IN 1778, SEVERAL YEARS into the Revolutionary War, a state constitutional convention in Massachusetts wrote a charter that explicitly denied free blacks—as well as Indians and mulattoes—the right to vote. Massachusetts citizens rejected the constitution, partly because of its racially discriminatory suffrage provision and its failure to eliminate slavery. Two years later Massachusetts approved a different constitution, which made no mention of black disfranchisement and declared that "all men are born free and equal."

In 1781 Nathaniel Jennison, a white farmer, attempted to reclaim the services of his slave, Quock Walker, who had deserted him to work on a nearby farm. When Walker resisted, Jennison severely beat him. Walker then sued Jennison for assault and battery, claiming that he was not, in fact, a slave. Jennison, in turn, sued his neighbor for attempting to entice away his slave. The state of Massachusetts criminally prosecuted Jennison for his attack on Walker.

Antislavery activists used the litigation to challenge the legality of slavery—under natural law, the Bible, and the "free and equal" provision of the 1780 constitution. Lawyer Levi Lincoln (later President Thomas Jefferson's attorney general) asked the Supreme Judicial Court of Massachusetts, "Can we expect to triumph over Great Britain, to get free ourselves until we let those go free under us?" Lincoln also appealed to natural law: enslaved blacks and free whites "all had one common origin, descended from the same parents, are clothed with the same kind of flesh, had the same breath of life—have the same common Saviour."

In 1783 Chief Justice William Cushing presided over the criminal prosecution of Jennison. Cushing instructed the jury that even though slavery had been established by custom in Massachusetts, it could no longer exist because sentiments "more favorable to the natural rights of mankind, and to that innate desire for liberty which Heaven, without regard to complexion or shape, has planted in the human breast—have prevailed since the glorious struggle for our rights began."

The natural rights ideology of the Revolution, the contributions made by black soldiers, and the economic forces set in motion by the war put slavery on the road to extinction in northern states. By 1790 Massachusetts no longer had any slaves.

White Europeans brought African slaves to the American colonies soon after their founding, though not in large numbers. In the early seventeenth century, northern colonies had as many slaves as southern ones. At this early date slaves did not work in large gangs on plantations, but rather performed many of the same tasks as white laborers. Indeed slavery was simply one end of a spectrum consisting of varying degrees of bound labor. Indentured servants, who were mostly white, could be bought, sold, and disciplined just like slaves. Until the mid-eighteenth century, as much as half of the laboring population of some colonies was legally not free. Upper-class whites tended not to sharply distinguish between black and white laborers, regarding both groups as immoral, shiftless, and indisposed to work except under coercion.

Around 1700 two factors led to an explosion in the slave populations of the southern colonies: a decrease in the supply of white indentured servants from England and a fall in black mortality rates. Tobacco cultivation, which dominated the economy of the Chesapeake Bay region, required a large labor supply, and planters increasingly turned to slaves, who constituted 7 percent of Virginia's population in 1680, 28 percent in 1700, and 46 percent in 1750. In South Carolina, where slaves mainly grew rice and indigo, they were 17 percent of the population in 1680, 44 percent in 1700, and over 60 percent by 1720.

As slave populations rapidly grew, living conditions became harsher. This generation of slaves worked harder, died earlier, and had less opportunity to accumulate property, establish a family, or gain freedom. Imported slaves were relatively cheap, and southern planters made little effort to provide them with decent food, clothing, or shelter. Greater violence was necessary to maintain the increasingly oppressive system of plantation slavery.

As southern society became more dependent on slavery, slave codes became more restrictive. Not only were slaves denied the rights to contract and own property, but some states made it a crime for owners to allow slaves discretion over the use of their time. Slave codes often barred slaves from learning to read and write, congregating in large numbers, owning firearms, and traveling without a pass. Slaves—and usually free blacks as well—were not permitted to testify in court against whites. Over time, colonial legislatures made it harder for owners to manumit their slaves, out of fear that free blacks would encourage slave rebellions and were likely to become public charges. Slaves who killed whites were not allowed to mitigate murder charges by pleading provocation, as the law refused to recognize that anything a white person said or did to a slave could legally excuse the use of deadly force.

Because of the need to maintain social control, only minor punishment—if any at all—was imposed on those who killed slaves, and even then only in cases of torture or extreme cruelty. To ensure the slave's complete submission to the master, the law imposed no liability on owners who killed slaves in the course of administering discipline.

Most owners at least occasionally whipped their slaves because they believed that proper discipline required it. Plantation overseers, who as short-term employees did not share the slave owners' interest in preserving the slaves' long-term health, were frequently crueler. Slave patrols were authorized to whip slaves who were discovered away from their plantations without a pass and to kill those who resisted authority. Masters had a legal right to track down escaped slaves with vicious dogs, even if the slaves died as a result.

The law generally treated slaves as property: they could be mortgaged and seized by creditors to satisfy a debt. For purposes of criminal punishment, however, slaves were treated as creatures of free will who were responsible for their actions. Slaves accused of capital offenses were formally tried and, if convicted, were usually executed, often through barbaric methods, such as burning or drawing and quartering. Less serious crimes were usually handled more informally on the plantation or through local justices of the peace, and punishment tended to be swift and harsh, often involving physical disfigurement, such as branding or ear lopping.

One of the most inhumane aspects of slave law was its treatment of families. Many owners allowed their slaves to "marry," but the law did not recognize such unions. Conscientious owners tried to avoid separating spouses from one another and parents from their children, but many owners did not. Even those who tried to keep families together were occasionally forced by financial exigencies to break them up, and no colonial slave code restricted their ability to do so during their lifetimes. The law sometimes favored keeping families together in estate or bankruptcy sales, but exceptions were afforded where family preservation would cause "material prejudice" to heirs or creditors. Slave children living in the Upper South had a roughly 50 percent chance of being separated from their parents before reaching adulthood.

To be sure, the law required masters to provide food and clothing to slaves, including in their old age, and many owners far exceeded the law's demands, regarding slaves as part of their families and treating them with benevolent paternalism. Female house slaves frequently developed intimate relationships with white mistresses and their children, whom they often nursed and helped to raise.

Moreover, laws restricting the freedom of slaves were frequently followed in the breach. Owners often gave slaves Sundays off and allowed them to hire themselves out on their own time; such practices hardened into customs, which then became difficult for owners to repudiate. Legal restrictions on educating slaves or permitting them to congregate for social events were often ignored in practice. Especially in cities, slaves enjoyed great mobility, acquired marketable skills, and were afforded relative freedom in allocating their time.

Most northern colonies had substantial slave populations. Around 1750, slaves constituted 15 percent of New York's population, 12 percent of Rhode Island's, and 8 percent of New Jersey's. As late as the Revolutionary War, 10 percent of New York's population and 6 percent of Rhode Island's was still enslaved.

Few northern slaves toiled in plantation agriculture. Those who worked on farms often labored beside whites, and many acquired the skills necessary to become independent farmers. In northern cities slaves worked in taverns, on ships, and as artisans and house servants. They were permitted to acquire property, and some achieved a moderate prosperity, occasionally even purchasing their own freedom. Because slaves in the North did not work in large gangs on isolated plantations, they were gradually assimilated to the languages, customs, and religions of their masters.

The slave codes of northern colonies were usually somewhat less draconian than those of the South. People who killed or maimed slaves were liable for the same punishments as if their victims had been white. However, after the New York slave insurrection of 1712, in which nine whites died before it was brutally suppressed, several northern colonies imposed tighter restrictions on slaves and free blacks, limiting their mobility and their rights to congregate and carry firearms. Fear of slave insurrections led many colonies to impose heavy taxes on the foreign slave trade, though the British government usually vetoed such measures. Northern colonies also adopted tougher restrictions on slave manumission, reasoning that free blacks were, as the Pennsylvania legislature put it, "an idle and a slothful people ... [who] often prove burdensome to the neighborhood and afford ill examples to other Negroes."

By the mid-eighteenth century, slavery was coming under assault in Pennsylvania, a state with a large Quaker population. In the early 1700s Pennsylvania Quakers had been as likely to hold slaves as anyone else, though they generally opposed the international slave trade and insisted that owners educate their slaves so they could study the Bible. By the 1750s, however, Quakers in Pennsylvania had condemned slavery, partly because they interpreted the French and Indian War then raging on the western frontier as divine retribution for the sins of slaveholding. In the following two decades, Quakers throughout the North condemned slavery.

The escalating conflict between the colonies and Great Britain over taxation and imperial control profoundly influenced American slavery. In 1774 the General Assembly of Rhode Island ended the importation of slaves, observing that "those who are desirous of enjoying all the advantages of liberty themselves, should be willing to extend personal liberty to others." In 1775 Thomas Paine, reflecting the view of many colonists, wondered how Americans could "complain so loudly of attempts to enslave them, while they hold so many hundreds of thousands in slavery?"

In 1776 Americans declared their independence to the world, proclaiming that "all men are created equal." The man who wrote those words—and many who read them—may not have thought that blacks were included. Thomas Jefferson, who owned well over one hundred slaves, believed that blacks were probably inferior to whites in reason and imagination and possibly of a different species. He also thought that "deep rooted prejudices entertained by whites" made it impossible for the two races to live together without "the extermination of the one or the other."

Yet Jefferson "trembled for his country when he remembered that God is just"—an allusion to his belief that slavery contravened natural law. Nor did Jefferson have much doubt as to what the future portended with regard to slavery: "Nothing is more certainly written in the book of fate than that these people are to be free." In 1779 Jefferson and other leading Virginians proposed a scheme for the gradual abolition of slavery in the state and the colonization of free blacks abroad.

Whether or not the founders thought blacks were "created equal," the Revolutionary War furthered the cause of emancipation. As the British military occupied coastal cities, thousands of slaves seized the opportunity to flee their masters. British promises to free those slaves who fought against the colonists pressured Americans to make similar guarantees. After initial hesitancy, both the Confederation Congress and many northern states allowed blacks into the Continental army and the state militias. In 1777 Connecticut passed a law easing the requirements for manumission in order to enable owners to free slaves so they could serve as "substitutes" in the Continental army. As many as five thousand blacks—most of them recently freed slaves—fought against the British in the Revolutionary War. After the war abolitionists promoted the cause of emancipation by commemorating blacks who had died in the fight for independence.

In 1780 the Pennsylvania legislature, observing that slavery was "disgraceful to any people, and more especially to those who have been contending in the great cause of liberty themselves," adopted the nation's first gradual emancipation scheme. The law

James Armistead (1748–1830), who spied for the Revolutionary Army

would free enslaved children who were born after the law's passage once they reached the age of twenty-eight. Permitting masters to maintain ownership of their current slaves and their slaves' children until they reached the age of maturity was seen as compensation for the invasion of property rights inherent in coerced emancipation. The law also contained permanent exemptions for slaveholding ambassadors and congressmen as well as a six-month exemption for out-of-state slave owners traveling through Pennsylvania with their slaves.

Several New England states quickly followed suit. In 1783 the Supreme Judicial Court of Massachusetts interpreted the "free and equal" clause of the state constitution to bar slavery. That same year slavery in New Hampshire was also ended by judicial decree. In 1784 legislatures in Connecticut and Rhode Island adopted gradual emancipation schemes.

In New York and New Jersey, however, where slave owners were more numerous and politically powerful, efforts to end slavery took longer to succeed. The national census of 1790 recorded well over 30,000 slaves still residing in those two states. New York did not adopt a gradual emancipation law until 1799, and New Jersey did not until 1804.

The Revolutionary War also induced a spate of slave manumissions in the Upper South. In 1782 the Virginia legislature authorized masters to emancipate slaves without receiving special permission from the government. Maryland and Delaware quickly adopted similar laws and debated proposals for gradual emancipation. In 1783 the Virginia legislature, reasoning that those who have "contributed towards the establishment of American liberty and independence should enjoy the blessings of freedom as a reward for their toils and labours," freed slaves who had served as substitutes for their masters in the Continental army. Virginia's free black population exploded as a result of these laws, increasing from 2,800 to over 12,000 in just eight years. Virginia statesmen spoke optimistically of the gradual abolition of slavery. In 1786 George Washington wrote that he hoped "to see some plan adopted, by which slavery in this country may be abolished by slow, sure, imperceptible degrees."

The Confederation Congress also debated antislavery measures. In 1784 Thomas Jefferson proposed an ordinance to bar slavery after 1800 from all territories under federal control. This measure faced strong southern opposition, and ultimately failed by a single vote. Its practicability seems doubtful, given that owners had already taken thousands of slaves across the Allegheny Mountains and that Virginia and North Carolina had ceded their western lands to Congress on the condition that slavery be permitted there.

In the summer of 1787, as the Constitutional Convention met in Philadelphia, the Confederation Congress passed an ordinance barring slavery from the Northwest Territory. This measure was uncontroversial. Even southern delegates supported it, probably because of the implicit quid pro quo that slavery would be permitted in southwestern territories and because some southern planters wished to avoid competition from slave labor in the Northwest.

This ban on slavery in the Northwest ultimately proved crucial; white southerners were the first to populate the region in large numbers and would likely have brought slaves with them had the law permitted. Had slave states emerged from this territory, as might have happened were it not for the Northwest Ordinance, the history of slavery in antebellum America might have been very different.

In May 1787 delegates assembled in Philadelphia to revise the nation's organic document. Under the Articles of Confederation,

Congress had lacked adequate power to raise revenue and regulate foreign commerce, and state governments had enacted debtor relief laws and inflationary monetary policies that elite statesmen tended to regard as officially sanctioned theft. While slavery had nothing to do with the calling of the convention, it played an enormous role in the proceedings.

American slavery was in transition in 1787. A couple of northern states had eliminated it; others were gradually doing so; and still others had defeated the efforts of abolitionists. Several northern delegates to the Philadelphia convention, including Benjamin Franklin and Alexander Hamilton, played prominent roles in their states' antislavery movements. Many southern delegates—including James Madison, George Mason, and Edmund Randolph of Virginia—regarded slavery as a temporary evil to be eliminated as soon as practically possible. Yet South Carolina and Georgia, hugely dependent on slave labor and voracious in their appetite for additional slaves, sent delegates to Philadelphia who defended slavery as a positive good and did not share the hope that it would eventually be abolished.

There was never any chance that the Philadelphia convention would write an antislavery constitution. Most northern states still had significant numbers of slaves, and even antislavery northerners believed in the sanctity of property rights. Furthermore most white northerners feared the creation of a large population of free blacks. Most important, northern delegates aspired to create a permanent union with southerners, who would never have agreed to an antislavery constitution.

Still, most of the delegates in Philadelphia were queasy about tainting the nation's organic document with linkages to slavery—an institution that many of them believed to contravene natural law. James Madison, one of the leading figures at the convention, acknowledged that it would be "wrong to admit in the

[19]

Constitution the idea that there could be property in men." Thus, the framers wrote a document that never mentions slavery by name, instead using euphemisms, such as "other persons."

In a sense they were writing two separate constitutions. As practical politicians who understood that slavery would not disappear any time soon, they wrote a constitution that protected the interests of slave owners. As idealists who were not oblivious to their historical reputations, they wrote a constitution that would require little amendment should slavery one day be abolished, as many of them hoped and expected that it would be.

The slavery-related battles at the Philadelphia convention were not over whether the Constitution should bar slavery or empower Congress to do so, but over how much power slave owners should have within the Union. As Madison repeatedly observed, the real divergence of interest at the convention was not that between large and small states; it was that between states with large and small slave populations. Thus, Madison proposed apportioning one house of Congress according to free population and the other according to free-plus-slave population.

Partly because the North and the South had different degrees of dependency on slave labor, they had conflicting economic interests. Southerners mainly produced agricultural staples—tobacco, rice, and indigo—for export to Europe, which inclined them to support free trade. The North had many more shippers, merchants, and nascent industrialists, who favored various mercantilist restrictions on trade. These conflicting sectional interests had nearly torn the Union asunder in 1786–87. Thus, northern and southern delegates came to Philadelphia suspicious of one another and determined to secure as much power as possible for their states within the new national government.

In 1787 the five southern states had almost precisely the same population as the eight northern states, if slaves were counted.

Therefore, if slaves were treated the same as free persons for purposes of apportioning representation in the House, the North and South would have equal power. If slaves counted for less, however, the South would be outnumbered.

Delegates from South Carolina and Georgia insisted that slaves should count equally for apportionment purposes: women and children counted even though they were not allowed to vote, so why should slaves not count as well? Moreover, slaves comprised a large portion of the South's wealth, and in 1787 many people still believed that wealth deserved as much consideration as population in determining representation.

Some northern delegates responded that slaves should not count for apportionment purposes, since unlike women and children, slaves were considered property. Elbridge Gerry of Massachusetts argued that if slaves counted for apportionment purposes, then cattle and horses should as well. Moreover, if southern states did not count slaves in apportioning representation in their own legislatures, they should not count for Congress's apportionment.

The debate grew heated. A compromise was proposed: slaves would count as three-fifths of free persons for apportionment purposes. Gouverneur Morris of Pennsylvania resisted the compromise as contrary to human nature and as likely to encourage the South to import more slaves. At one point the convention voted to reject the compromise, and the southern delegates threatened to walk out. William Davie of North Carolina declared that his state "would never confederate on any terms that did not rate [slaves] at least as three fifths," and he warned that if northern states refused to count slaves at all in apportioning the House, then "the business was at an end." Not to be outdone, Morris responded that the people of his state would "never agree to a representation of [slaves]" and that if sectional divisions were as great as southerners were claiming, then it might be best if the North and the South "take a friendly leave of each other."

Morris was bluffing, however, and the delegates eventually agreed to the compromise: slaves would count three-fifths for purposes of apportioning representation in the House but also for purposes of allocating those taxes that the Constitution required to be apportioned according to population. At the state ratifying conventions, this compromise proved uncontroversial. Only in subsequent decades, as southern candidates regularly won presidential elections, did northerners raise protests against the three-fifths clause (which increased southern representation in the electoral college as well as the House).

A second issue concerning slavery vexed the convention. Delegates from South Carolina and Georgia strongly opposed restrictions on the foreign slave trade. These states had lost tens of thousands of slaves during the Revolutionary War and wanted to increase their supply without paying inflated prices from states such as Maryland and Virginia, which had already become exporters of slaves to the Deep South. At the convention, George Mason of Virginia attacked the slave trade as "infernal traffic." A skeptical South Carolinian replied that Virginia would "gain by stopping the importations" because "[h]er slaves will rise in value, & she has more than she wants." Northern delegates objected to the foreign slave trade both because it contravened "the most sacred laws of humanity" and because it heightened the risk of slave insurrections, which the national government would bear the costs of suppressing. Delegates from the Deep South again threatened to walk out.

This controversy, too, proved susceptible to compromise. Earlier in the convention, southern states had resisted granting Congress the power to regulate interstate and foreign commerce because they believed such authority would principally benefit northern manufacturers and shippers. Southern delegates had insisted that Congress be permitted to pass commercial legislation only if a two-thirds majority concurred, thus giving the South a functional veto.

With the convention deadlocked over the issue of the foreign slave trade, a deal was negotiated: South Carolina delegates would drop their demand that commercial legislation be subject to a supermajority voting requirement. In exchange, delegates from New England states, which benefited financially from the transport of both foreign slaves and the goods produced by slave labor, agreed to a constitutional provision barring Congress from interfering with the foreign slave trade for twenty years. In addition the South received a constitutional provision forbidding export taxes, which southerners had feared could be used to indirectly attack slavery by taxing the goods it produced. A narrow majority of states approved this compromise, which eventually enabled South Carolina to import nearly one hundred thousand additional slaves before 1808, when Congress finally terminated the foreign slave trade.

The last of the slavery-related provisions to make it into the Constitution caused far less controversy. Late in the convention's proceedings, two delegates from South Carolina proposed a provision entitling slave owners to the recovery of escaped slaves. Precedent for such a measure existed in the Northwest Ordinance, and the proposal elicited little opposition from northern delegates, who respected property rights in slaves and whose states for the most part still had significant slave populations.

Returning home from the Philadelphia convention, some southern delegates bragged that they had secured a strongly proslavery document. Charles Cotesworth Pinckney told his fellow South Carolinians, "In short, considering all circumstances, we have made the best terms for the security of this species of property [slaves] it was in our power to make. We would have made better if we could; but on the whole, I do not think them bad."

Abolitionists in the North seemed to agree. One of them, Samuel Hopkins, asked in despair, "How does it appear in the sight of Heaven that *these states*, who have been fighting for liberty…, cannot agree in any political constitution, unless it indulge and authorize them to enslave their fellow men!" Concurring with this assessment, a later group of abolitionists denounced the Constitution as a "covenant with death" and an "agreement with hell."

Yet, some northern delegates insisted that the Constitution had put slavery on the road to extinction. James Wilson told the Pennsylvania ratifying convention that the constitutional provision authorizing Congress to terminate the foreign slave trade after twenty years laid "the foundation for banishing slavery out of this country." Moreover, Wilson insisted, the formation of new states was within the control of Congress, and "slaves will never be introduced amongst them." Such claims were not absurd: many of the Founding generation genuinely seem to have believed that authorizing the abrogation of the foreign slave trade and constraining the physical expansion of slavery by keeping it out of the Northwest Territory would ultimately ensure its demise.

Whoever had the better of this debate, it is hard to see what additional antislavery actions the framers could have realistically taken. The South would not have joined a union in which slave property was insufficiently protected. And for northerners to form a union without the South would have done nothing to quicken the extinction of slavery there.

CHAPTER TWO

The Antebellum Period

In March of 1854 Sherman M. Booth, a white abolitionist newspaper editor from Milwaukee, Wisconsin, obstructed the capture and return of an alleged fugitive slave being held in federal custody near Racine. An angry mob, which Booth had helped to agitate, seized the black man, Joshua Glover, and helped spirit him away to Canada.

Booth and other leaders of the mob were convicted in federal court of violating the Fugitive Slave Act of 1850, which criminalized the obstruction of fugitive slave renditions. In an extraordinary act of defiance, the Wisconsin Supreme Court freed Booth on the ground that the federal law was unconstitutional, despite rulings by several federal courts that it was not. Furthermore, the Wisconsin jurists tried to subvert the U.S. Supreme Court's effort to take jurisdiction over Booth's case by refusing to certify the record for appeal. The state legislature implicitly endorsed this insurrectionary judicial behavior by passing a statute that would have effectively nullified enforcement of the federal fugitive

Sherman Booth (1812–1904), abolitionist newspaper editor

slave law in Wisconsin by granting alleged fugitives a jury trial and paying the costs of their defense.

In 1859 the U.S. Supreme Court chastised the Wisconsin judges for their recalcitrance and laid down the law on federal supremacy. Undeterred, the Wisconsin legislature responded by purporting to nullify the high court's decision on the ground that states—not federal courts—were the final arbiters of the federal constitution. The governor of Wisconsin briefly contemplated using the state militia to liberate Booth from federal custody. Though he ultimately backed down, a mob stepped in to accomplish the same objective.

Booth himself quickly became a political hero in Wisconsin, traveling around the state campaigning for Republican Party candidates. The lawyer who had defended him was elected to the Wisconsin Supreme Court, while the one judge on that court who had failed to support Booth's appeal lost his seat.

By 1859 antislavery northerners regarded the U.S. Supreme Court as the tool of southern slave owners. The *Milwaukee Sentinel* declared, "Nobody any longer entertains respect for the Supreme Court, because in its legal decisions it has clearly violated every principle of right and justice, and rendered itself a mere machine for the advancement of the interests of one section of the country." Northerners increasingly regarded the federal fugitive slave law as evil, and they were no longer willing to be accomplices in its enforcement.

White southerners, in turn, were beginning to wonder if it was worth having a union with people who behaved this way. When abolitionists in 1851 forced their way into a federal courtroom in Boston and helped a fugitive slave escape to Canada, a newspaper in Richmond, Virginia, warned that the Union could not "survive many such shocks." When southerners seceded from the Union in 1860–61, one of their principal grievances was northern nullification of the Fugitive Slave Clause. Robert Toombs of Georgia charged Wisconsin specifically with being "smeared with the blood of a violated Constitution."

The escalating controversy over fugitive slave renditions illustrates how a nation that was half slave and half free was torn asunder by sectional differences involving slavery.

Although northern states had ended slavery in the decades following the Revolutionary War, the freedom that blacks enjoyed in the North was often very limited. Congress had banned slavery in the Northwest Territory, but territorial legislatures authorized long-term indentures of blacks, usually for as long as twenty to forty years. Much like slaves, indentured blacks could be bought and sold, and their children automatically became indentured until the age of twenty-eight or thirty. Free blacks living in these territories (later states) could not vote, testify in cases involving whites, or serve on juries or in the militia.

The national government did not regard free blacks as fit for citizenship. The nation's first naturalization law, adopted in 1790, was limited to whites. In 1792 Congress restricted enrollment in the state militias to whites, and in 1810 it barred blacks from serving as U.S. postal carriers. Beginning in the 1820s, several U.S. attorneys general authored legal opinions denying that free blacks could be American citizens.

Free blacks in the North lived in constant fear of kidnapping and enslavement. As the market value of American slaves soared in the early nineteenth century—a result of a cotton boom and Congress's termination of the foreign slave trade—the incidence of such kidnappings increased dramatically. Congress repulsed pleas from antislavery groups for federal antikidnapping legislation or for greater procedural safeguards in the federal fugitive slave law. Some northern states proved more receptive and adopted laws requiring slave catchers to bring alleged fugitives before magistrates for more elaborate hearings than federal law contemplated.

In *Prigg v. Pennsylvania* (1842), the U.S. Supreme Court struck down one such state law on the ground that it obstructed the right of owners to recapture fugitive slaves. The Court ruled unconstitutional any state law that "interrupts, limits, delays or postpones the right of the owner to the immediate possession of the slave." The master's rights must absolutely prevail over the interest of northern states in protecting free blacks from kidnapping.

The justices in *Prigg* probably believed they were bolstering the Union by vindicating a right that southern slaveholders had come to regard as part of the "sacred compromise" of 1787. Preserving the Union came at the expense of northern free blacks.

At the time of the Founding, many Americans—both northerners and southerners—had assumed that slavery would gradually wither away. Subsequent events proved them badly mistaken. The invention of the cotton gin in the 1790s made cotton production enormously profitable, just as tobacco cultivation was becoming much less so. Between 1790 and 1800, South Carolina's annual cotton exports increased from less than ten thousand pounds to roughly six million.

In addition, while the founders had kept slavery out of the Northwest Territory, they had permitted it into the Southwest. Kentucky and Tennessee entered the Union as slave states in the 1790s. Opponents of slavery made only halfhearted attempts to bar it when Congress organized the Mississippi Territory in 1798. In 1802 Georgia ceded its western land claims to Congress on the condition that slavery be permitted there.

In 1803 President Thomas Jefferson negotiated the Louisiana Purchase with Emperor Napoleon of France, thus doubling the geographic size of the United States. Roughly 30,000 slaves already lived in this territory, and Congress rejected proposals to restrict slavery there. Native American tribes residing in the Louisiana Purchase territory were gradually exterminated or expelled, clearing the path for white pioneers, who brought more slaves with them. Several additional slave states soon entered the Union: Louisiana in 1812, Mississippi in 1817, and Alabama in 1819. The domestic slave trade transported enormous numbers of slaves from east to west—about 120,000 in the 1810s and 300,000 in the 1830s—though many thousands died during the trek.

Changes in slave law reflected the rising market value of slaves and the South's growing dependence on slave labor. For the first time, several states defined the malicious killing of a slave by a third party as murder. States also increased the punishment for nonfatal abuse of slaves by third parties, and some states made the theft of slaves a capital offense. More elaborate procedural protections were afforded to slaves charged with capital offenses: rights to counsel, grand jury indictment, jury trial, and appeal.

The rising value of slaves generally translated into better treatment, as owners had strong incentives to preserve the value of their property. Indeed, masters insisted that slaves in the South were better treated than free industrial workers in Europe or the North. In terms of material conditions alone, those claims have some merit. American slaves tended to work fewer hours than the European proletariat, they were better fed, and they were better cared for in youth, sickness, and old age. Because of decent material conditions, the American slave population increased tenfold between the termination of the foreign slave trade and the Civil War. In the Southwest, however, where slaves tended to work in large gangs on enormous plantations, the institution of slavery became more rigid, discipline was more brutal, and mortality rates were higher.

As well as southern slave owners felt they treated their slaves, they still lived in constant fear of slave revolts. The few revolts that occurred—and even those that were aborted—had a profound effect on the legal treatment of slaves and free blacks.

In the summer of 1800, a planned slave insurrection led by Gabriel Prosser, an enslaved blacksmith, was foiled in Richmond, Virginia. Twenty-six blacks were hanged in response. Soon thereafter, the Virginia legislature passed a law requiring manumitted slaves to leave the state within a year of receiving their freedom. Conscientious slave owners now found it difficult to free their slaves because of the expense of staking them to new lives in the North and the necessity of dividing slave families. Reflecting widespread anxiety over the rapid growth of the state's free black population, the Virginia legislature also endorsed the colonization of free blacks overseas.

Another slave insurrection was aborted in Charleston, South Carolina, in 1822. Whites blamed free black sailors from the West

Indies for encouraging the slave revolt planned by Denmark Vesey, a free black man. Thirty-five blacks were executed, and the state legislature adopted a black seaman's law, which several other southern states soon emulated. This law required that free black sailors serving on ships docked in Charleston harbor be locked up in the city jail for the duration of their visits. The ship owner or captain was liable for the sailors' maintenance while incarcerated. Should that obligation not be satisfied by the time the ship sailed, the black sailors were to be sold into slavery.

A free black citizen of the British Empire from Jamaica challenged this law, which South Carolina justified on self-defense grounds. Justice William Johnson of the U.S. Supreme Court invalidated the statute, but South Carolina continued to enforce it for decades, despite periodic protests from the British government. Two of President Andrew Jackson's attorneys general agreed with South Carolina that the law was a permissible exercise of state police power and that free blacks did not have constitutional rights.

As slavery gradually died in the North and was replaced by a system of free labor, many northerners grew concerned that slavery seemed to be thriving in the South and indeed was spreading to the West. When settlers in the Missouri Territory petitioned to enter the Union with a proslavery constitution in 1819, northern congressmen tried to condition statehood on the abandonment of slavery. They simultaneously sought to bar slavery from the Arkansas Territory. A crisis over the Union ensued, as southerners decried the constitutionality of these proposals and threatened secession should they become law.

A compromise was negotiated. Maine, which petitioned for statehood around the same time, was admitted as a free state. Missouri entered the Union as a slave state. The remainder of the

Louisiana Purchase territory was divided by a line drawn at 36° 30' latitude, with slavery barred to the north and permitted to the south.

The Missouri Compromise was a patchwork settlement, grounded in an exercise of congressional power that southerners had just been insisting was unconstitutional. Yet it succeeded in suppressing controversy for the next quarter of a century, mainly because it resolved the fate of all territory then in the federal government's possession.

Most northerners who supported restricting the spread of slavery did not wish to abolish it in the South, nor did they endorse racial equality. Almost all northerners conceded that southerners had property rights in slaves that warranted protection and that the federal government lacked constitutional power to interfere with slavery in existing states. Moreover, they sought to restrict the expansion of slavery mainly because they wished to preserve the West for whites, not because they cared about the welfare of blacks.

In 1817 growing anxiety among whites over the nation's burgeoning free black population led to the founding of the American Colonization Society, which was committed to promoting the voluntary removal of blacks from the United States. The society deemed free blacks "notoriously ignorant, degraded and miserable, mentally diseased, [and] broken[]spirited." Colonizers argued that blacks would never be permitted to vote, sit on juries, or attend school with whites because of innate racial prejudices, and that because blacks were unfit for competition with whites, their condition would continue to deteriorate. Educating them would be pointless because it would simply give them a taste for privileges they could never attain.

Supporters of colonization included many of America's most illustrious statesmen—James Madison, Henry Clay, Daniel

Webster, and John Marshall. In the 1820s many northern state legislatures urged Congress to appropriate funds for colonization. South Carolinians threatened disunion should Congress even debate such proposals. But colonization was probably never a feasible option: the expense of relocating millions of blacks to Africa would have been exorbitant, and most colonizers were not prepared to use the coercion that would have been necessary to impel most blacks to leave the country that they regarded as their home.

Antislavery sentiment in the North assumed a new dimension with the publication in 1831 of William Lloyd Garrison's *Liberator* and the founding two years later of the American Antislavery Society. Unlike previous opponents of slavery, the abolitionists denounced colonization, demanded the *immediate* abolition of slavery, and endorsed full racial equality. Their ranks gradually expanded, due to the spread of evangelical Christianity and the growth of capitalism and its free labor ideology, which regarded slavery as anathema.

In the 1830s, however, abolitionists were a tiny percentage of the northern population—and an extremely unpopular one. They were physically assaulted; their printing presses were destroyed; and in 1837 one of them was murdered. Opponents despised abolitionists for their racial egalitarianism and accused them of jeopardizing the Union.

Reasoning that any racially discriminatory laws provided fodder for slavery's defenders, abolitionists sought to purge them all. In 1843 Massachusetts abolitionists convinced the state legislature to repeal the ban on interracial marriage. Though they failed to persuade legislators to forbid racial segregation in railroad transportation, abolitionists successfully lobbied railroad companies to end that practice. In the late 1840s abolitionists unsuccessfully litigated against racial segregation in Boston's public schools.

To be sure, many abolitionists drew the color line at social equality. They would not invite blacks into their homes or churches and sometimes not even into their antislavery societies, partly because of prejudice and partly because they did not want to alienate more northern whites than absolutely necessary. Many blacks charged white abolitionists with hypocrisy for preaching racial equality while refusing to hire blacks for nonmenial positions at their Wall Street firms.

Abolitionist support for racial equality helped foster antiblack riots, which were common in the antebellum North. Between 1830 and 1850, white mobs on five different occasions attacked black homes and churches in Philadelphia. Many of the rioters were recent Irish immigrants, who competed with free blacks—usually successfully—for menial jobs. As the great black abolitionist Frederick Douglass observed, "Every hour sees us elbowed out of some employment to make room perhaps for some newly arrived immigrants, whose hunger and color are thought to give them a title to especial favor."

When northern blacks sought to improve themselves through education, white resistance could be ferocious. In 1832 a Quaker woman, Prudence Crandall, admitted a black student to the boarding school for girls that she had established in Canterbury, Connecticut. When most of the white students promptly withdrew, Crandall decided to operate the school exclusively for black girls. The town erupted in protest: "A school for nigger girls" would depreciate property values and attract blacks to Canterbury.

When Crandall's school opened its 1833 session with fifteen or twenty black students, mostly from out of the state, townspeople turned to harassment. The school was denied necessary provi-

Prudence Crandall (1803–1890)

sions; its water well was made unusable with manure; and the village doctor refused to treat sick pupils. The Connecticut legislature passed a law requiring the consent of local authorities in order to operate a school for black children from out of state. Crandall was convicted of violating this statute. After continued harassment, including an effort to burn down her house, she finally abandoned the project.

The legal status of free blacks in the North deteriorated as Jacksonian Democrats celebrated the equality of all white men. In 1821 New York's constitutional convention eliminated property qualifications for white voters while preserving a hefty one for blacks. Pennsylvania's constitutional convention of 1837 disfranchised blacks entirely. Delegates explained that blacks were "a debased and degraded portion of our population" and that permitting them to vote would "invite the black outcasts and worthless vagrants, of other states, to settle among us." As public education spread throughout the North in the 1830s, blacks were either denied access altogether or racially segregated in inferior schools. Courts rejected legal challenges to segregation on the ground, as an Indiana court put it, that "black children were deemed unfit associates of whites."

In 1838 a visitor to Philadelphia observed that free blacks were "marked as the Hebrew lepers of old. They are not slaves indeed, but they are pariahs; debarred from all fellowship save with their own despised race." The brilliant French observer Alexis de Tocqueville, who visited the United States in the early 1830s, concluded that racial prejudice was stronger in the North than in the South, and he predicted that free blacks would eventually be either exterminated or expelled.

White southerners argued that the degraded status of northern free blacks proved, in the words of leading slavery apologist George Fitzhugh, that "humanity, self-interest, consistency, all require that we should enslave the free Negro." A southern congressman contrasted "the happy, well-fed, healthy, and moral condition of the southern slaves, with the condition of the miserable victims and degraded free blacks of the north."

Yet, no matter how badly free blacks were treated in the North, they were not bought and sold, barred from traveling, or prevented from forming families. They also had the right to organize in protest of their conditions—something that southern blacks were not permitted to do. It was for good reason that northern free blacks almost never sold themselves into slavery.

In the summer of 1831, Nat Turner, a slave preacher, led the most deadly slave revolt in American history. About fifty-five whites—mostly women and children—were murdered in Southampton County, Virginia, before the insurrection was brutally suppressed. Scores of blacks were summarily and indiscriminately executed. Southern whites tended to blame abolitionists for the death and destruction. William Lloyd Garrison received numerous death threats, and the Georgia legislature posted a reward of $5,000 for his arrest.

"The bloody massacre" in Southampton, in the words of the *Richmond Enquirer*, "raised the floodgates of discussion" on slavery, leading the Virginia legislature to debate proposals for the gradual emancipation and colonization of slaves. Whites in western Virginia had long condemned slavery for eroding the state's soil, degrading white labor, and inhibiting foreign immigration. Nat Turner's revolt induced many whites in the slave-heavy counties of eastern Virginia also to consider gradual emancipation. After lengthy debates, however, the legislature narrowly rejected such proposals. Virginians were simply too deeply invested in slavery; compensated emancipation for half a million slaves was not financially feasible; and very few free blacks volunteered to be colonized.

Turner's rebellion also inspired a legislative crackdown on free blacks and slaves. Many southern states passed laws barring free blacks from owning firearms, congregating in large numbers, and preaching. In some states free blacks accused of crime lost their right to a jury trial. The two southern states that still permitted free blacks to vote now disfranchised them. Many states banned the immigration of free blacks, and some politicians called for the expulsion of free blacks from the South.

Legislatures enacted new measures banning the teaching of slaves to read and write and forbidding slaves from leaving plantations without a pass. Legislative bans on property holding by slaves were now enforced more rigorously. Courts refused to execute trusts or deeds providing money to slaves for their comfort and protection.

Southern courts and legislatures restricted in-state manumission of slaves, reasoning that the hope of emancipation inspired dangerous thoughts among slaves and that the presence of free blacks incited slave insurrections. In addition, as white southerners came to regard slavery as a positive good rather than a necessary evil, easy access to manumission became harder to justify: why reward meritorious service by freeing slaves, who were better off enslaved?

The ideology of slavery as a positive good became dominant in different places at different times. In the 1830s most white Virginians still saw slavery as a necessary evil, while South Carolinians tended to see it as a positive good. As northern abolitionists attacked southern slaveholders as evil, more white southerners became convinced that slavery was good: it civilized slaves, Christianized them, and provided care and nurturing during their youth, sickness, and old age. When the 1840 census seemed to confirm that the further north free blacks lived, the more likely they were to be denominated as "insane and idiots," southerners such as John C. Calhoun saw proof that emancipation would be "a curse instead of a blessing" for slaves and that slavery should be expanded rather than restricted.

Growing differences between the North and the South over slavery bled into national politics on the issues of fugitive slave renditions and slavery in the federal territories. Feeling increasingly assailed over slavery, white southerners demanded greater security from the federal government. In turn, northerners grew resentful of the aggressive southern "slave power," and they resolved to resist its encroachments.

In 1845–46, southern slave owners, determined to expand their slave empire into Texas, incited a war with Mexico. In response northerners of all political persuasions sought to bar slavery from any territory acquired as a result of that war. In 1850 southern slave owners realized their ambition for a more stringent federal fugitive slave law. Northerners were so repulsed by scenes of terrified fugitives being dragged in chains back to slavery—sometimes with the assistance of federal officers—that they supported obstruction of the law's enforcement.

In 1854 white southerners induced a Democratic-controlled Congress to allow slavery into the Kansas Territory, where it had previously been barred. Outraged northerners deserted the Democratic Party in droves, and they formed the Republican Party, whose principal commitment was to limiting the expansion of slavery. In 1857–58, when southern slave owners sought to force a proslavery constitution on an antislavery majority in Kansas, enough northerners became Republicans that three years later the party was able to elect a president with virtually no southern support.

As northerners lost patience with the growing demands of southerners, they ceased making accommodations to slavery. Northern legislatures and courts began to free slaves whose owners had voluntarily brought them along on trips to the North. Many northern states also enacted laws to protect free blacks from kidnapping. Because these measures impeded the rendition of fugitive slaves, they violated the spirit—and perhaps the letter—of the Court's ruling in *Prigg*.

The growth of antislavery sentiment occasionally enabled abolitionists to make headway against racial prejudice. In 1849, when the Free Soil party held the balance of power in the Ohio legislature, it tried to repeal a portion of the state's discriminatory black code. In 1855 antislavery legislators in Massachusetts enacted the nation's first ban on racial segregation in public schools.

Yet most opponents of slavery expansion were racists, who wished to bar slavery from western territories in order to preserve the region for whites. Pennsylvania congressman David Wilmot, author of the famous proviso that would have barred slavery from the territories acquired in the war with Mexico, assured his House colleagues that he had no "morbid sympathy for the slave" but rather was pleading "the cause and the rights of white freemen," who deserved a country in which they could "live without the disgrace which association with negro slavery brings upon free labor." An Ohio representative who favored keeping slaves out of the western territories explained, "God has ordained, and no human law can contravene the ordinance, that the two races shall be separate and distinct."

The Republican Party did little to promote the interests of free blacks. Abraham Lincoln explained that Republicans wanted slavery excluded from the territories so they could become "the homes of free white people." To be sure, Lincoln occasionally focused attention on the Declaration of Independence, which he thought plainly encompassed blacks within the notion that "all men are created equal." More frequently, though, Lincoln insisted that he had never been "in favor of bringing about in any way the social and political equality of the white and black races." He observed, "There is a physical difference between the two [races], which in my judgment will probably forever forbid their living together upon the footing of perfect equality." So long as both races remained in the United States, "there must be the position of superior and inferior, and I as much as any other man am in favor of having the superior position assigned to the white race."

In 1848 Lincoln's home state of Illinois banned black migration. Indiana, Iowa, and Oregon quickly followed suit. Senator Stephen Douglas of Illinois defended these prohibitions on the ground that northern states should not become "an asylum for all the old and decrepit and broken down Negroes that may emigrate or be sent to [them]." Bans on black migration enjoyed overwhelming popular support; Indiana voters approved theirs by a margin of eight to one. Courts sustained such measures as conducive to the good of both races. Many proponents of black exclusion also endorsed the colonization of free blacks to Africa—a movement that enjoyed a renaissance of public support in the 1850s.

By 1860 blacks could vote without racial restriction only in five New England states, which together contained just 6 percent of the North's free black population. Massachusetts remained the only state to bar school segregation or to allow blacks to sit on juries. Abolitionist efforts to repeal bans on black testimony in court failed in all but one of the five states that had them. Throughout the North, places of public accommodation either excluded or segregated blacks.

In the South the legal treatment of free blacks and slaves grew even harsher. Many states barred in-state manumissions of slaves entirely, and by 1860 some even forbade out-of-state manumissions by testamentary disposition, reasoning that slaves freed in the North could still facilitate slave escapes in the South. In the 1850s many southern states instituted new colonization schemes, and they became less fastidious about requiring the consent of those being colonized. In 1858, Edmund Ruffin, a leading pro-slavery theorist from Virginia, proposed a solution to the "great and growing evil" of free blacks who were "idle, profligate, and dishonest" and exercised a "corrupting influence on slaves": they should either be reenslaved or else expelled from the state.

In 1859 Arkansas became the first state to pass a law threatening to enslave free blacks who did not leave within a year. John Brown's raid at Harper's Ferry later that year supplied new urgency to demands for black expulsion, and two other southern state legislatures passed such measures, only to have them vetoed by governors. Other southern states legally assimilated free blacks to slaves. In 1861 Georgia adopted a presumption that all laws enacted with reference to slaves also applied to free blacks. Under this law, free blacks were barred from education, denied the right to assemble or keep firearms, and subjected to search without warrant and trial without jury, except in capital cases.

In 1857 the U.S. Supreme Court gave its imprimatur to such legal treatment of free blacks. Writing for the majority in *Dred Scott v. Sandford*, Chief Justice Roger B. Taney declared that the framers of the Constitution had regarded blacks "as beings of an inferior order, and altogether unfit to associate with the white race, either in social or political relations; and so far inferior, that they have no rights which the white man was bound to respect." Accordingly the Court ruled that free blacks did not qualify as citizens of a state for purposes of federal constitutional protection.

Dred Scott (1795–1858), painted by Louis Schultze, commissioned by a "group of Negro citizens," and presented to the Missouri Historical Society in 1882

After *Dred Scott,* the State Department denied passports to free blacks seeking to travel abroad, and the commissioner of the General Land Office ruled that blacks had no right under federal statute to purchase public lands on which they had made improvements. Southern whites who favored evicting free blacks also invoked *Dred Scott* as authorization. Republicans generally shied away from criticizing the Court's ruling on black citizenship because northern opinion was so hostile to racial equality. Democrats, attacking "Black Republicans" for their "foul doctrine of admitting a nigger into your family to marry your daughters, and to be your social and political equal," made gains in six of the seven northern states holding elections in the fall of 1857.

Dred Scott also—more famously—invalidated the Missouri Compromise on the ground that Congress lacked the power to bar slavery from federal territories. This aspect of the ruling was hugely controversial, as it condemned as unconstitutional the principal plank in the platform of the newly formed Republican Party. Republican newspapers railed against the Court as "a propagandist of human slavery." They compared Chief Justice Taney's opinion unfavorably to that which could have been written by "any slave driving editor or Virginia barroom politician," and they declared that the decision was proof "of a grand conspiracy against freedom" that sought to make slavery "the law of the Republic." By contrast, Democratic newspapers praised the Court for offering an "olive branch" that would save the nation from "fanaticism and sectionalism." They insisted that "the court has spoken and their [sic] position must be accepted," and they warned that Republican criticism of the ruling was "brim full of the elements of sedition, treason, and insurrection."

In the years between the Founding and 1860, northerners first ended slavery in their own states, then began to resist the efforts of southerners to use the national government to defend and expand the "peculiar institution." Yet rising antislavery sentiment in the North did not translate into greater racial egalitarianism. In 1857 Abraham Lincoln observed that the "ultimate destiny" of free blacks "has never appeared so hopeless." Growing legal proscription and the heightened risk of kidnapping under the 1850 Fugitive Slave Act induced as many as 10 percent of the 200,000 blacks living in the North to migrate to Canada in the 1850s. In 1860 it would have been impossible to predict that within a decade slavery would be dead and blacks would be granted the civil and political rights of citizens.

CHAPTER THREE

The Civil War and Reconstruction

ON JULY 13, 1863, a mob consisting largely of lower-class white Irishmen began a four-day rampage in New York City. The immediate cause of the violence was the federal draft law, which had just gone into operation in the city. In the days before the riot, Democratic newspapers and politicians had assailed the draft as unprecedented and unconstitutional. The editor of the *New York Daily News* had objected to this "strange perversion of the laws of self-preservation which would compel the white laborer to leave his family destitute and unprotected while he goes forth to free the negro, who, being free, will compete with him in labor."

The principal targets of the mob included the office of the provost marshal (who administered the draft), the office of the antislavery *New York Tribune,* and the black orphans' asylum. Blacks were dragged off of city streetcars and beaten, and some were lynched. Armed Irish youngsters wandered the streets, declaring that they "wanted to find some Niggers to shoot." The *New York Times* blamed the riot on Democrats, who had lashed the mob into a frenzy with warnings that "they were about to be dragged unlawfully into the field, to be killed for the benefit of the niggers."

Troops fresh off the Gettysburg battlefield were called in to suppress the disorder. More than one hundred people lost their lives in the violence. It was the deadliest urban riot in American history, and it showed how resistant many white northerners were to converting a war for the Union into a crusade to end slavery and establish racial equality.

Fearing the threat to slavery posed by the election of a Republican president, seven southern states seceded from the Union

NEW YORK—HANGING AND BURNING A NEGRO IN CLARKSON STREET.

New York City draft riot—*Hanging and Burning a Negro in Clarkson Street*

during the winter of 1860–61. Four more joined them after President Abraham Lincoln called seventy-five thousand militiamen into federal service in response to the Confederates' assault on Fort Sumter in April 1861. Majority opinion in the North refused to countenance the destruction of the Union without a fight, but most northerners initially were not seeking to end slavery.

Since its inception in 1854, the Republican Party had denied that the national government had power to control slavery in the states. Early in 1861, as a last-ditch effort to keep the South in the Union, Congress passed a constitutional amendment that would have forever barred Congress from interfering with slavery in the states. The Civil War interceded before the requisite number of states could ratify it, but this measure nearly became the thirteenth amendment to the Constitution.

In his first inaugural address, Lincoln reiterated that he had neither the inclination nor the power to interfere with slavery in existing states and that he was duty bound to enforce the fugitive slave law. In a special message to Congress in July 1861, Lincoln reaffirmed that he had "no purpose, directly or indirectly, to interfere with slavery in the States where it exists." Later that month both houses of Congress passed resolutions reaffirming that the war's objective was to preserve the Union, not to interfere with slavery. As late as the summer of 1862, Lincoln repeated this point:

> If I could save the Union without freeing *any* slave I would do it; and if I could save it by freeing *all* the slaves I would do it; and if I could do it by freeing some, and leaving others alone I would also do that. What I do about slavery, and the colored race, I do because I believe it helps to save the Union; and what I forbear, I forbear because I do *not* believe it would help to save the Union.

Despite such repeated assurances, the objectives of the war soon expanded to include the abolition of slavery. As the toll in death and destruction rose to astonishing proportions, northerners resolved to abolish the institution that they deemed responsible. As one Republican congressman explained, "the mere suppression of the rebellion will be an empty mockery of our sufferings and sacrifices, if slavery shall be spared to canker the heart of the nation anew, and repeat its diabolical deeds." As Union troops penetrated deeper into the South, slaves took matters into their own hands, fleeing their plantations and seeking protection from the Union army.

As the war dragged on, Congress took action against slavery. Late in the summer of 1861, Congress authorized the confiscation of slaves whose labor was being used by Confederate military forces. Early in 1862 it abolished slavery in the District of Columbia, paying compensation to loyal owners. Ignoring *Dred Scott*, Congress terminated slavery in federal territories. It also instructed Union officers to cease returning fugitive slaves to their owners, and it authorized the enrollment of slaves in the Union army, granting them their freedom in exchange.

Early in the war, Lincoln had opposed a policy of general emancipation. Four border states that permitted slavery had remained in the Union, but their loyalty was precarious. Lincoln worried that any significant antislavery actions by the federal government would drive those states into the Confederacy. He is supposed to have said that while he would like to have God on his side during the war, he "must have Kentucky." In the summer of 1861, Lincoln reversed an order of General John C. Fremont that had purported to free the slaves of disloyal owners in Missouri. Lincoln feared that Fremont's order would "alarm our Southern Union friends, and turn them against us—perhaps ruin our rather fair prospect for Kentucky."

Yet by the summer of 1862, Lincoln was contemplating a change in policy. In July he wrote that the enemies of the Union "must understand that they cannot experiment for ten years trying to destroy the government, and if they fail still come back into the Union unhurt." Lincoln knew that emancipating slaves would deprive the South of its principal labor force. If freed slaves were then enrolled in the Union military, the North's manpower advantage would be considerably augmented. In addition, converting the war into a crusade against slavery would deter England and France, both of whom had long condemned slavery, from intervening on the side of the Confederacy, as they might otherwise have been inclined to do. Yet, even as he leaned toward emancipation, Lincoln continued to support the colonization of freed slaves outside of the United States.

In September 1862 Lincoln issued his preliminary Emancipation Proclamation, which declared that in one hundred days, slaves would be emancipated in those states still in rebellion, though not in areas already occupied by Union troops. Abolitionists celebrated the proclamation as "an act of immense historic consequence," and Republican newspapers defended it as a "perfectly legitimate and perfectly proper" war measure.

However, Democratic newspapers and politicians thought the measure grossly unconstitutional, and they condemned Lincoln's conversion of the war into an antislavery crusade. The Union's leading general at the time, George B. McClellan, called the proclamation "infamous" and told his wife that he would not "fight for such an accursed doctrine as that of a servile insurrection." A Democratic editor in Ohio denounced the proclamation as "monstrous, impudent, and heinous...insulting to God as to man, for it declares those 'equal' whom God created unequal." The president of the Confederacy, Jefferson Davis, called the proclamation the "most execrable measure in the history of guilty man," and the Confederacy threatened to execute captured black soldiers.

Partly as a result of Lincoln's proclamation, the Republicans lost thirty-four congressional seats in the 1862 elections. They also lost control of several northern state legislatures, which promptly demanded retraction of the "wicked, inhuman and unholy" proclamation as their price for continued support of the war. Democratic charges that emancipation would induce a flood of black migration to the North and thus reduce the wages of white workers produced race riots in southern Ohio and Indiana and renewed efforts to enforce black exclusion laws in Indiana and Illinois.

Nonetheless, as the war became a crusade to end slavery and as roughly two hundred thousand blacks enrolled in the Union army, progressive racial change began to occur. Bowing to repeated protests, Congress eventually provided black soldiers with equal pay, uniforms, and equipment. Congress also repealed statutory bans on black postal carriers and the testimony of blacks in federal court. The U.S. Supreme Court admitted the first black lawyer to practice at its bar.

Black military service generated greater support for black suffrage. In January 1865 blacks in Nashville petitioned a convention of Tennessee Unionists: "The Government has asked the colored man to fight for its preservation and gladly he has done it. It can afford to trust him with the vote as it trusted him with the bayonet." Many northern cities desegregated their streetcars during the war, and in the year the war ended, Massachusetts passed the first state law forbidding racial discrimination in public accommodations. Soon thereafter, a couple of northern states barred school segregation.

The Emancipation Proclamation was not the final word on slavery, both because of doubts as to whether the president had the constitutional authority to free slaves by executive order and because the proclamation did not cover the border states or those portions of the Confederacy already under Union military control. To complete the abolition of slavery, a constitutional amendment would be necessary.

By the summer of 1864, a Republican Party that was badly divided over how far to expand the rights of freedmen easily coalesced behind a constitutional amendment forbidding slavery. But Congress divided along partisan lines over the proposed amendment, and House Republicans lacked the two-thirds majority necessary to pass it.

Timely battlefield victories by General William Tecumseh Sherman in Georgia and General Philip Sheridan in the Shenandoah Valley enabled Republicans to win a massive victory in the congressional elections that fall. The antislavery amendment was now certain to pass when the new Congress convened in December 1865. Not willing to wait that long to put the final nail in the coffin of slavery, President Lincoln twisted enough Democratic arms to narrowly secure passage of the amendment during Congress's lame duck session in January 1865. Charges of vote buying tainted the amendment in the minds of white southerners for more than a generation.

The scope of the Thirteenth Amendment's prohibition on "slavery and involuntary servitude" aroused great controversy. During congressional debates, Democrats warned that the amendment would call into question antimiscegenation laws, and they almost universally voted against it. After the amendment's passage, however, Democrats argued that it simply forbade the buying and selling of people and the expropriation of their labor. When ratifying the amendment, some southern legislatures added provisos to clarify that abolishing slavery did not mean an end to white supremacy. The existence of black codes in the antebellum

North lent credence to this claim. Northern states that had abolished slavery long ago denied blacks the rights to vote, serve on juries, testify against whites in court, and attend public schools.

Nearly all Republicans had a broader conception of what ending slavery entailed. They believed that the Thirteenth Amendment guaranteed blacks, at a minimum, basic civil rights—the rights to contract, own property, legal protection, and court access. Some Republicans went further, arguing that the abolition of slavery automatically conferred upon blacks the full rights of citizenship, including the rights to vote and hold office. Abolitionists such as Senator Charles Sumner of Massachusetts held the broadest conception of the amendment—that it barred all racial distinctions in law, including segregation and bans on interracial marriage. Ultimately, most congressional representatives voting for the amendment were embracing an antislavery principle rather than carefully parsing the amendment's legal implications.

Yet the question of scope quickly became important. By the end of 1865, southern states were enacting laws designed to ensure that blacks remained a subordinate agricultural labor force. These "black codes" required freedmen, on threat of vagrancy prosecutions, to sign annual agricultural labor contracts. They also provided for the apprenticing of black children, with or without the consent of their parents. Other measures sought to bolster the supply of black agricultural labor, while constraining the demand for it, by denying blacks the right to buy land outside of cities, restricting the access of blacks to nonagricultural vocations, and criminalizing efforts by one employer to entice away another's workers.

Southern blacks suffered from more than just legal oppression: white vigilantes declared open season, maiming and murdering blacks without legal repercussions. In 1866 politically motivated violence in Memphis and New Orleans killed scores of blacks. Between 1865 and 1868, Texas whites killed a thousand blacks.

After winning a devastating war against slavery, Republicans were not going to permit white southerners to functionally re-enslave blacks. Nor were they willing to permit the southern political structure to remain essentially intact, thus creating a risk of future civil wars. While President Andrew Johnson and northern Democrats might be willing to readmit southern states to Congress once they had ratified the Thirteenth Amendment, Republicans insisted on their doing more.

Early in 1866 congressional Republicans proposed civil rights legislation to confer citizenship upon blacks and to guarantee them the same rights as whites to contract, own property, sue in court, and benefit from legal protection. Yet President Johnson and most Democrats challenged the constitutionality of the proposed bill. Prior to the Civil War, it would have been relatively clear that Congress lacked the authority to forbid states from discriminating against people based on their race. To be sure, the Thirteenth Amendment had expanded congressional power by conferring the authority to enforce the amendment's ban on slavery. But Democrats denied that Congress had been empowered to confer citizenship or to forbid race discrimination with regard to civil rights.

Even some Republicans doubted that the Thirteenth Amendment authorized such civil rights legislation, and they proposed the Fourteenth Amendment to remove all doubts. Section one of that amendment forbids states from denying persons equal protection of the law; abridging the privileges or immunities of citizenship; or taking life, liberty, or property without due process of law. Section five authorizes congressional enforcement. Together, these two sections of the Fourteenth Amendment would clearly empower Congress to enact the proposed civil rights bill.

Whether the amendment was intended to go further than this has generated great controversy—both then and ever since. Most Republicans embraced a three-part conception of rights—civil, political, and social—and argued that the amendment protected only civil rights, such as contract and property ownership. Political rights such as voting, and social rights such as racial integration, were beyond the amendment's scope. Democrats, seeking political advantage by exaggerating the amendment's reach, charged that it would forbid school segregation and bans on interracial marriage. Comprehending the limits of their constituents' racial tolerance, most Republicans dismissed these claims as absurd. Even some of the more radical Republicans conceded that the amendment did not protect black suffrage.

The Fourteenth Amendment also addressed issues of political reconstruction. Republicans faced a quandary: their party did not exist in the South before the Civil War, and its hold on national power was tenuous after the war because Democrats remained competitive in the lower North. Even worse, the South, which had generally dominated antebellum national politics, was now due more than a dozen additional congressional seats because, with the abolition of slavery, blacks would count as whole persons for the apportionment of the House—whether or not they were permitted to vote, as apportionment is based on persons, not voters.

Republicans were determined to prevent the resurgence of a political party that they regarded as treasonous. By enfranchising blacks, who were 40 percent or more of the population in eight southern states, and by disfranchising some whites who had supported the Confederacy, Republicans could establish a political base in the South. Their difficulty, however, was that northern whites seemed intensely resistant to black suffrage. Between 1860 and 1867, roughly a dozen northern states and western territories rejected black suffrage in referendum votes—mostly by overwhelming margins.

Because Republicans feared that directly enfranchising blacks would cost them seats in the 1866 congressional elections, they acted by indirection. Section two of the Fourteenth Amendment provides that states that disfranchise adult male citizens for reasons other than crime or participation in rebellion must suffer a reduction in their congressional representation proportionate to the percentage of adult males disfranchised. For example, South Carolina, with a black population of roughly 60 percent, would have lost three-fifths of its congressional representation had it persisted in disfranchising blacks. But northern states, with black populations averaging only 1 or 2 percent, could continue to disfranchise blacks without penalty. Section three of the amendment barred many former Confederates from holding state or federal office until Congress suspended the ban.

These were ingenious—if perhaps hypocritical—methods of establishing a southern base for the Republican Party and preventing the former slavocracy from reassuming power. But the success of these measures depended on the ratification of the Fourteenth Amendment, and only one of the former Confederate states ratified it in 1866. Without significant support from the South, the amendment could not possibly be approved by three-quarters of the states, as required for ratification.

The 1866 congressional elections, which took place only in the North, were widely deemed a referendum on the Fourteenth Amendment and resulted in a huge victory for Republicans. But southern states still refused to ratify the amendment. Congressional Republicans then took matters into their own hands. Invoking the congressional war power, which continues to operate beyond the cessation of hostilities, they passed the 1867 Reconstruction Act, which appointed military governors to oversee southern state governments, enfranchised southern blacks, and used federal troops to register them. The law also required southern states to hold constitutional conventions which, in turn, would be required to enfranchise blacks and hold elections to form new governments. Those southern whites barred from office under section three of the Fourteenth Amendment were prohibited from voting in the elections for delegates to state constitutional conventions.

Most of the southern states held such conventions in 1867–68. Republicans dominated, and many of the delegates were black. When new state governments were elected under the new constitutions, Republicans remained in control. In the summer of 1868, most of these governments ratified the Fourteenth Amendment. Democrats assailed the legality of this process: Congress had destroyed existing state governments, forcibly reconstructed them, and then required them to ratify the Fourteenth Amendment as a condition of regaining their congressional representation. But congressional Republicans had the votes, and they declared the amendment lawfully ratified. For generations, white southerners regarded the amendment as illegitimate because of the unorthodox procedures that had produced its ratification.

In the South black suffrage was now protected in three ways: state constitutional provisions, the penalties mandated by section two of the Fourteenth Amendment on states that disfranchised blacks, and congressional readmission conditions that barred southern states from subsequently disfranchising existing voters. However, none of these safeguards for black suffrage was particularly reliable. Should Democrats regain power, state constitutions were easily amended. Southern whites might happily accept a reduction in their congressional representation in exchange for regaining control over local politics. And even many Republicans doubted the constitutionality of congressional readmission conditions.

In the North most states still barred blacks from voting. In 1868 the Republican Party's platform defended black suffrage in the South but insisted that "the question of suffrage in all the loyal States properly belongs to the people of those States."

In a stunning repudiation of their party platform, congressional Republicans used the lame duck session of Congress that convened after the 1868 elections to pass the Fifteenth Amendment, which bars disfranchisement based on race. Apparently, Republicans found the results of those elections too close for comfort. Ulysses S. Grant was elected president with just 53 percent of the popular vote. Republicans suffered heavy losses in congressional races, and the party's two-thirds majority in the House was in jeopardy. Republicans may have calculated that the time for a constitutional amendment protecting black suffrage was now or never.

Democrats screamed bait and switch. But by strict party-line votes, Republicans pushed the amendment through Congress and the requisite number of state legislatures. In a few northern states, voters punished Republicans for breaking their promise not to impose black suffrage on the North by electing Democratic state legislatures. But when those legislatures tried to rescind their predecessors' ratifications of the Fifteenth Amendment, congressional Republicans denied that they had the power to do so. The four southern states not yet represented in Congress were required to ratify the Fifteenth Amendment as a condition for readmittance.

Because amending the Constitution is so onerous, most successful amendments have enjoyed the support of overwhelming popular majorities. By contrast, the Fifteenth Amendment was likely opposed by a majority of Americans. It was adopted because the majority wing of the majority party willed it. Because white southerners viewed the process by which the amendment was adopted as illegitimate, they felt morally justified in evading it.

The scope of the Fifteenth Amendment is narrow: it forbids disfranchisement based on "race, color, or previous condition of servitude." It does not explicitly bar literacy tests, poll taxes, or property qualifications—all of which would have adversely impacted blacks. Many congressional Republicans had favored a broader amendment to enfranchise all adult males except for convicted criminals. But New England Republicans, worried about enfranchising Irish Catholic immigrants, and West Coast Republicans, worried about enfranchising Chinese immigrants, blocked the broader proposal. Similarly, efforts to expand the amendment to forbid race discrimination in office holding foundered because many northern Republicans in Congress believed their constituents would rebel at the thought of blacks holding office. The narrow scope of the final version of the amendment seemed to invite southern circumvention.

With their suffrage rights secured, southern blacks voted in huge numbers and helped to elect Republican state governments throughout the South. Black voters also elected large numbers of black officeholders. At times during Reconstruction, blacks comprised nearly half the lower-house delegates in Mississippi and Louisiana, and a majority in South Carolina. Sixteen southern blacks served in Congress, many held state executive offices, and a black justice sat on the South Carolina Supreme Court. Thousands of blacks held local office as sheriffs, magistrates, county councillors, and school board members.

Reconstructed state governments repealed bans on black jury service, and many juries had black members. The new state constitutions extended public education to blacks for the first time. Though schools nearly everywhere in the South remained racially segregated, as long as blacks voted in large numbers, their schools tended to receive equal funding. Republican state governments dramatically increased spending on other public services, such as orphanages and institutions for the physically and mentally disabled.

Group portrait of African American congressional representatives
in 1872

Blacks reached the pinnacle of their political power in the
South in 1873–74, when black office holding peaked and several states banned race discrimination in public accommodations.
Partly as a reward to southern black voters, congressional Republicans passed a federal public accommodations law in 1875.

Despite such impressive accomplishments, Reconstruction
delivered far less to blacks than they had hoped. Many freedmen
had anticipated that Congress and the reconstructed state governments would confiscate the property of slave owners who had
tried to destroy the Union and redistribute it to them. However,
proposals for redistribution, put forth by Congressman Thaddeus
Stevens among others, came to naught, as most Republicans were

too conservative in their views of property rights to support land redistribution. After the war, most southern blacks continued to work for whites as tenant farmers or sharecroppers. Undoubtedly they were better off free than enslaved, but their immediate economic prospects were dismal.

Furthermore, the gains that southern blacks did make during Reconstruction were precarious. Southern whites attacked and destroyed black schools whenever federal troops were unavailable to protect them. The Ku Klux Klan intimidated blacks from voting. In most of the South, blacks were badly outgunned. If they did fight back, they were usually slaughtered.

In the short term, racial atrocities in the South appalled white northerners and unified congressional Republicans. In 1870–71, Congress imposed severe penalties for private violence interfering with federal rights and authorized the president to suspend the writ of habeas corpus and to use military force to suppress electoral violence. The Justice Department, with the aid of the army, arrested hundreds of Klansmen in 1871–72, prosecuted and convicted dozens of them, and temporarily shut down the Klan in several southern states.

Yet the political participation of southern blacks depended on the continued willingness of the national government to devote resources to suppressing white vigilante violence. That will soon faltered, and Reconstruction came to a close.

CHAPTER FOUR

Retreat from Reconstruction

ON EASTER SUNDAY, 1873, one of the largest massacres of blacks in American history took place in Grant Parish, Louisiana. Black Republicans and white Democrats had each claimed victory in a disputed local election. Blacks occupied the local courthouse for weeks, before a mob of several hundred whites, armed with a cannon, attacked and routed them. More than one hundred blacks were killed, many of them executed in cold blood after surrendering.

Because the killings were racially motivated and occurred in connection with an election dispute, the federal government claimed jurisdiction to prosecute. Ninety-eight whites were indicted under recently enacted federal legislation that made it a crime to interfere with federal rights. Only nine people were actually prosecuted, and just three were convicted.

In March 1876 the Supreme Court overturned those convictions on a technicality: the indictment charging the defendants had not explicitly stated that the alleged interference with voting rights had been racially motivated—even though the indictment *did* generally describe a racial massacre. Furthermore, the justices found no "state action," as required by the Fourteenth Amendment, to support the counts of the indictment charging denials of due process and equal protection—even though public officials had participated in the slaughter.

By 1876 Reconstruction was all but dead. Supreme Court justices showed no inclination to revive it. Even had they possessed the desire to do so, they probably lacked the power.

At the same moment that southern states were enacting civil rights legislation and electing record numbers of blacks to political office, many northern whites were losing their enthusiasm for Reconstruction. Some were troubled by the antidemocratic implications of sustained military rule in the South and others by the centralization of authority in the hands of the federal government. A yearning for sectional reconciliation also induced many northern whites to abandon Reconstruction. A severe economic recession beginning in 1873, combined with rising class conflict in northern cities, diverted attention from issues of racial equality and sapped the resources necessary for continued federal intervention to protect the rights of southern blacks. Many northern whites had never believed that blacks were qualified to participate in politics, and they looked for any excuse to abandon the experiment.

As early as 1872, an elite group of "Liberal" Republicans, appalled by the "ignorance and degradation" of the reconstructed southern governments and determined to restore the "better class" of white southerners to political power, urged amnesty for former Confederates and an end to military rule in the South. Although President Grant easily won reelection that year and mainstream Republicans retained control of Congress, they too had supported widespread amnesty in order to preempt the appeal of the Liberals. By the end of 1872, the Justice Department had largely abandoned prosecutions of Klansmen. In his second inaugural address, President Grant proclaimed the former Confederate states "happily rehabilitated," and he emphasized the need for reconciliation rather than additional Reconstruction measures.

The congressional elections of 1874 were a massive repudiation of the Republican Party. To be sure, issues other than Reconstruction played some role: the economic recession, the corruption of the Grant administration, and the president's supposed desire for a third term. But Reconstruction issues were dominant.

Congressional Republicans had recently been trying to enact a civil rights bill that would guarantee blacks "full and equal enjoyment" of public accommodations, common carriers, and schools. Democrats made the bill a principal issue in the elections, asking voters, "Do you wish to be buried in a nigger grave-yard? Do you wish your daughter to marry a nigger? Are you going to send your boy to a nigger school?" In Tennessee the Republican gubernatorial candidate attributed his defeat to the thousands of hill-country whites who had remained loyal to the Union during the Civil War but now swore "that they would never again vote with a party which supported the coeducation of the races." The civil rights bill also contributed to Republican losses in southern Ohio and Indiana, where large numbers of blacks resided and schools were rigidly segregated.

"The Republican Party Struck by Lightning," declared one Republican newspaper. Another called the result "not merely a victory but a revolution." In one of the most dramatic shifts in congressional history, a 110-seat Republican majority in the House turned into a 60-seat deficit. Republicans also lost control of two more southern state governments and several northern ones.

Control of the House would enable Democrats to block funding for the enforcement of existing civil rights legislation and prevent the passage of any additional measures. Many Republicans, including the president, now concluded that Reconstruction was dead. The *Chicago Times* exhorted Republicans to quickly "solve the 'southern problem,' by withdrawing [the national government's] meddlesome agencies of every kind from the political affairs of the southern states, remitting them wholly to the management of their people."

Meanwhile, southern whites were using deadly violence to "redeem" their states from Republican control. The Grant administration had sporadically used military force and criminal prosecutions to suppress such violence. But now, northern voters—and, with them, the administration—had lost the will to suppress what the president called these "annual, autumnal outbreaks in the South."

The critical contest came in Mississippi in the fall of 1875. White Democrats, promising to "carry the election peaceably if we can, forcibly if we must," went on a rampage, murdering dozens of blacks. Earlier that year, the Grant administration had been stung by criticism when it used federal troops to prevent Democrats from assuming contested seats in the Louisiana legislature. Now, Grant and his Cabinet explicitly weighed the costs and benefits of dispatching troops to rein in the electoral violence: they could possibly preserve Republican rule in Mississippi, but they risked alienating northern white voters who wanted Reconstruction to end.

Grant and his colleagues decided to abandon Republicans in Mississippi in order to enhance the electoral prospects of Republicans in Ohio, where there was a gubernatorial election that fall and where the 1876 presidential contest was likely to be determined. Freed from external constraints, white Democrats suppressed the black vote in parts of Mississippi and redeemed the state. Republican Rutherford B. Hayes narrowly won the Ohio governorship and then the presidency the following year.

Six months after the Grant administration permitted a racial slaughter to occur in Mississippi, the U.S. Supreme Court freed the perpetrators of the Grant Parish massacre. Most newspapers, even in the North, applauded the decision. The *New York Herald* agreed with the justices that "it is high time for a return to constitutional limits." The *New York Times* observed, "Ten years ago the North was nearly united in a feeling of sympathy for the freedmen, and in a determination to defend their rights. Now ... not a few believe that the rights of the whites have been infringed upon." The *Atlanta Daily Constitution* approvingly noted that "the advent of a democratic house of representatives and the improved tone of public sentiment, have impelled the court to do what it could no longer decently avoid doing."

In another ruling the same day, the Court invalidated a federal statutory provision that criminalized the refusal of election officials to receive lawfully cast ballots. The Court reasoned that this provision was not explicitly limited to *racially motivated* refusals to accept votes and that Congress had no generalized authority to protect voting rights. The justices easily could have sustained this provision by construing it to require a racial motive, but in 1876, they were not inclined to strain to uphold civil rights legislation. The country had given up on Reconstruction, and so had the Court.

If Reconstruction was not yet completely dead, it soon would be. In 1876 Republican Rutherford B. Hayes, campaigning for the presidency on a platform of sectional reconciliation, promised to restore to the South "the blessings of honest and capable local self government"—code words for ending Reconstruction.

The election was closely fought and the results fiercely contested. The Democratic candidate, Governor Samuel Tilden of New York, won several northern states and all of the southern states that had already been redeemed from Republican rule.

That put him within a single electoral vote of winning the presidency.

But the election results in the three unredeemed southern states—Florida, Louisiana, and South Carolina—were hotly disputed. Rampant fraud and violence, including the murder of scores of blacks, had marred the contest in these states. Both sides claimed victory, but Republican state election officials dutifully decreed their candidate—Hayes—the winner.

Democrats cried fraud and threatened to march on Washington and reignite the Civil War. To avert bloodshed Congress—with Democrats controlling the House and Republicans the Senate—appointed a commission to determine who was entitled to the contested electoral votes. That commission consisted of five members of the House, five senators, and five Supreme Court justices. Even if the commission's elected officials voted along party lines, as expected, it was hoped that the justices might transcend partisanship. That hope proved naive. The commission divided eight to seven along party lines and awarded all of the contested electoral votes to Hayes. The decisive ballot was cast by Justice Joseph P. Bradley, a Republican.

Once again, Democrats protested that they were being cheated. Agents representing Hayes consulted with southern leaders, many of whom cared more about regaining control of state governments than about winning the presidency. A deal was negotiated: in exchange for Hayes becoming president, he would admit a southern Democrat to the Cabinet and remove federal troops from the South.

Within weeks of Hayes's assuming the presidency, the last Republican state governments in the South fell. The Republican Party had abandoned southern blacks, many of whom had risked their lives to make Hayes president. "The long controversy over the black man," observed the *Chicago Tribune*, "seems to have reached a finality."

Restored to power throughout the South, Democrats repealed public accommodations laws, formalized racial segregation in public schools, enacted measures constraining the mobility and bargaining power of black agricultural workers, and drastically reduced public spending on services such as education. They also adopted electoral devices—such as poll taxes, residency and registration requirements, and surrogate literacy tests—to suppress black voting and further reduce the strength of the Republican Party.

Yet well into the 1880s, blacks continued to vote in significant numbers in most southern states. So long as they voted, blacks continued to sit on juries, hold elected office, and enjoy roughly equal funding for their schools. At least some railroads and public accommodations continued to provide blacks with nonsegregated service.

The national government did not entirely abandon southern blacks after the 1876 elections. President Hayes was sincere when he said that the Civil War amendments must be "fully and fairly obeyed and enforced" despite the removal of federal troops from the South. In 1878 Hayes protested "Southern outrages," and his administration continued to prosecute perpetrators of electoral violence against southern blacks, though with increasingly little success.

After Democrats took control of both houses of Congress in 1878, they tried to repeal the statutes authorizing federal supervision of elections and criminalizing the deliberate exclusion of blacks from juries. Hayes repeatedly vetoed such efforts. In 1880 the Supreme Court, dividing along partisan lines, affirmed the constitutionality of the federal statute that proscribed race discrimination in jury selection. The Court also sustained broad federal power to protect the right to vote in *federal* elections.

Yet even Republican justices rejected social equality among the races and disfavored large expansions of federal power to protect the rights of blacks. In an 1883 trilogy of decisions, the Court gave its blessing to the end of Reconstruction.

In one ruling the Court barred the federal prosecution of a white man who had seized a black man from the custody of a sheriff and lynched him. The justices objected to the statutory provision under which the indictment was brought because it was not expressly limited to *racially* motivated interferences with federal rights. Rather than reading such a requirement into the statute to preserve its constitutionality, the justices freed the lyncher.

In a second ruling the Court unanimously upheld a state statute that imposed heavier penalties on fornication between parties of different races than that between parties of the same race. The justices reasoned that so long as the white and the black parties to interracial fornication were subjected to similar penalties, the races were being treated equally. This decision laid the analytical foundation for sustaining racial segregation, which also purported to extend equal—albeit separate—treatment to the races.

In the most important of the 1883 trilogy, the *Civil Rights Cases*, the justices invalidated the public accommodations section of the 1875 Civil Rights Act on the ground that the Fourteenth Amendment imposed limits only on actions of the *state* and thus Congress lacked the power to forbid discrimination in *privately* owned establishments. Justice Bradley wrote for the majority:

> When a man has emerged from slavery, and by the aid of beneficent legislation has shaken off the inseparable concomitants of that state, there must be some stage in the progress of

his elevation when he takes back the rank of mere citizen, and ceases to be the special favorite of the laws, and when his rights as a citizen, or a man, are to be protected in the ordinary mode by which other men's rights are protected.

A contrary ruling would not have been difficult to defend legally. The Thirteenth Amendment is not limited to state action, and the justices easily could have determined that race discrimination in public accommodations is one of the "badges or incidents" of slavery that the amendment can be interpreted to forbid. Moreover, places of public accommodation, which are licensed by public authorities and are generally open to all paying customers, are hardly the quintessentially private actors whom the Fourteenth Amendment immunized from constitutional regulation.

Yet in 1883 the justices, like most of the country, wished for a return to normalcy. Blacks must now protect their rights in the

Justice Joseph P. Bradley (1813–1892)

same way as other Americans—through their state governments. How they were to do this, given that southern states were suppressing black suffrage through fraud and violence, was not the justices' concern.

Blacks protested the ruling, comparing it to the infamous *Dred Scott* decision. Southern whites were predictably delighted; white men stood and cheered in the Atlanta opera house when the decision was announced. Public opinion in the North also generally endorsed the ruling. The *New York Times* nicely captured the prevailing sentiment: the principle involved in the case was "no longer an issue in national politics and can never again be made one." The Court's judgment was "but a final chapter in a history full of wretched blunders, made possible by the sincerest and noblest sentiment of humanity."

Blacks were not the only racial minority suffering oppressive discrimination at this time. Chinese immigrants were treated nearly as harshly in the West as blacks were in the South.

The Chinese came to California in large numbers during the gold rush in 1849 and then stayed to help build the Central Pacific Railroad. Over the next three decades, roughly 300,000 Chinese immigrants came to America, settling overwhelmingly on the West Coast. In 1860 Chinese were more than 9 percent of California's population.

Employers often preferred Chinese laborers to Caucasian ones because they worked for lower wages and did not join unions and participate in strikes. As early as 1852, resentful white workers passed resolutions protesting unfair competition by the Chinese. That year, California's governor called on the state legislature to restrict Chinese immigration. In 1855 the legislature enacted a tax of fifty dollars on each Asian immigrant, but the state supreme court invalidated it on the basis of U.S. Supreme Court precedent, which tightly constrained the ability of states to limit foreign immigration.

Most whites held racist stereotypes of the Chinese. In 1854 the California Supreme Court interpreted a state law forbidding testimony by blacks or Indians in cases involving white parties to also bar testimony by Chinese, whom the court deemed to be "a race of people whom nature has marked as inferior" and whose "mendacity is proverbial." In 1862 Governor Leland Stanford decried "the presence among us of a degraded and distinct people" and called for legislation to suppress Chinese immigration. The Chinese were frequently targets of vigilante violence. In October 1871 a white mob in Los Angeles shot, hanged, and burned to death eighteen Chinese. As aliens ineligible for citizenship under federal law, the Chinese could not vote. In 1870, when Congress for the first time made blacks eligible for citizenship through naturalization, it rejected efforts by Senator Sumner to make the Chinese eligible as well.

In 1878–79 several factors led a constitutional convention in California to adopt drastic anti-Chinese measures: the accelerating pace of Chinese immigration after the Civil War, the economic depression of the 1870s, and the growing political power of an anti-Chinese workingmen's party. The new state constitution barred the Chinese from public employment and from employment by private corporations. The constitution also instructed the legislature to adopt regulations necessary to protecting the state from dangerous aliens; cities were authorized to segregate the Chinese residentially. In 1885 the California legislature mandated school segregation for the Chinese, even though it had already barred segregation of blacks and Indians. Local ordinances sought to exclude the Chinese from various occupations.

At the behest of western congressional representatives, the federal government enlisted in this anti-Chinese crusade. Proponents of ending Chinese immigration argued that the Chinese were unfit for self-government, that they undercut the wages of white laborers, that their "heathen" customs led to debauchery, and that their filthy living conditions posed public health hazards. In 1882 Congress passed the Chinese Exclusion Act, which clarified that Chinese were ineligible for U.S. citizenship and barred immigration of Chinese laborers for ten years (a time limit that was subsequently extended and then made permanent in 1924, before being repealed during World War II). In 1888 Congress went even further, barring the reentry of Chinese laborers who had left the United States, even if they had received a government-issued certificate guaranteeing their right of return. In 1892 Congress required Chinese residing in the United States to secure certificates of lawful residency and authorized one year's imprisonment at hard labor and deportation for those failing to do so.

Dissatisfied with the federal government's efforts to limit Chinese immigration, mass meetings throughout the West demanded expulsion of the Chinese, and an epidemic of vigilante violence against them erupted. In September 1885 in Rock Springs, Wyoming, white coal miners went on a rampage against Chinese who had replaced them in the Union Pacific mines. Dozens of Chinese homes were torched, twenty-eight Chinese were killed, and several hundred more were driven from town. Soon thereafter, three Chinese were shot to death in western Washington, five were lynched in Idaho, and hundreds were violently expelled from mining towns throughout the Pacific Northwest. In 1887 thirty-one Chinese miners were robbed, murdered, and mutilated near the Snake River in Oregon. Prosecutors generally declined to bring criminal charges in such cases because obtaining convictions from all-white juries composed of local citizens would be impossible.

The U.S. Supreme Court intervened against only the most blatant forms of anti-Chinese discrimination. In 1886 the Court invalidated a San Francisco ordinance that required persons establishing laundries in wood buildings to secure permits from the board of supervisors. The ordinance specified no criteria to guide the supervisors' discretion, and in practice the board granted permits to essentially all Caucasian applicants and to no Chinese ones. This was race discrimination too blatant for the justices to overlook. Similarly, Justice Stephen Field, sitting as a circuit judge, invalidated San Francisco's "queue ordinance," which required prisoners to cut their hair short, as a transparently anti-Chinese measure. When Congress sought to deny jury trials to Chinese facing possible imprisonment at hard labor for alleged violations of immigration restrictions, the justices refused to acquiesce.

But courts generally approved more subtle anti-Chinese measures. In 1885 the justices unanimously sustained a San Francisco ordinance imposing a curfew on laundries, refusing to inquire into the legislature's motive, which had plainly been anti-Chinese animus. Lower courts, similarly declining to investigative the legislature's purpose, upheld anti-Chinese ordinances specifying minimum floor spaces for rooms in lodging houses and forbidding people on city sidewalks from carrying baskets attached to poles on their shoulders.

The Supreme Court sustained the Chinese Exclusion Act, even though Congress has no enumerated power to control immigration, reasoning that authority over aliens is inherent in national sovereignty. The Court then ruled that this inherent power was broad enough to authorize Congress to require Chinese to obtain certificates of lawful residency and even to renege on its promise to allow the reentry of Chinese laborers carrying certificates of return. The Court also sustained Congress's power to eliminate judicial review of the determinations by immigration officials of which Chinese aliens domiciled in the United States had rights of reentry after departure.

As the country gave up on Reconstruction, so did the Court. As the nation experienced convulsions of anti-Chinese prejudice, so did the justices. In the 1870s and 1880s, the Supreme Court did little to safeguard the rights of oppressed racial minorities.

CHAPTER FIVE

White Supremacy Ascendant

BY THE MID-1890S North Carolina was the only southern state not controlled by the Democratic Party. Blacks still actively participated in politics and held hundreds of local offices. In 1898, determined to rectify this "unnatural" state of affairs, white North Carolinians conducted a tumultuous political campaign under the banner of white supremacy. White newspapers carried sensational headlines announcing a rash of alleged rapes of white women by black men. In Wilmington, a city where blacks held dozens of public offices, a Democratic Party leader instructed his followers that if a black man tried to vote on election day, "kill him, shoot him down in his tracks."

A few days after the Democrats won a sweeping victory at the polls, several hundred whites in Wilmington burned down the office of a black newspaper editor, Alexander Manly, who had outraged southern whites by suggesting that many of the white women who accused blacks of raping them had actually been consensual

A mob stands in front of the destroyed newspaper office of Alexander Manly in Wilmington, North Carolina

sexual partners. The mob intimidated white Republican officials—derided as "White niggers"—into resigning their jobs and fleeing town. It attacked black neighborhoods, murdering a dozen blacks and driving nearly 1,400 of them out of the city. The wife of a former southern congressman, Rebecca Felton, defended the perpetrators: "[I]f it requires lynching to protect woman's dearest possession from drunken human brutes—then I say lynch a thousand a week if it is necessary!"

Black leaders pleaded with President William McKinley to denounce the atrocities and send federal troops to Wilmington. McKinley had been born into an abolitionist family, had served as a general in the Union army, and had strongly defended black voting rights as a U.S. congressman. But now he turned a deaf ear to appeals for his intervention.

Northern newspapers, rather than denouncing the racial massacre, blamed blacks for provoking it. The Spanish-American War earlier that year had, as the *Atlanta Constitution* explained, "seal[ed] effectively the covenant of brotherhood between the north and south and complete[d] the work of reconciliation which commenced at Appomattox." A black editor presciently observed that "the closer the North and South get together by this war," the more difficult it would become for blacks "to maintain a footing."

The new Democratic legislature of North Carolina promptly called a constitutional convention to disfranchise blacks. One of the leaders of the Wilmington riot conceded that the disfranchising proposal violated the federal constitution, but he insisted that "there aren't enough soldiers in the U.S. Army" to undo white political supremacy in North Carolina. In his second inaugural address in 1901, President McKinley ignored black rights and boasted of sectional reconciliation: "We are reunited. Sectionalism has disappeared."

White supremacy reemerged ascendant in the South around 1900. White southerners, who generally regarded the Fifteenth Amendment as "the greatest crime of the nineteenth century," used fraud and violence to nullify black voting and seize political control for the Democratic Party. Democratic legislatures enacted complex voter registration and residency requirements that further reduced black voting and Republican representation. State constitutional conventions consummated black disfranchisement by adopting poll taxes and literacy tests. Most blacks could not afford to pay a fee for voting, and literacy tests conferred nearly unfettered discretion on voter registrars, who used it to reject black registrants.

By the early 1900s, such measures had virtually eliminated black political participation in the South. In Louisiana black voter registration fell from 95.6 percent before the adoption of an 1896 registration law to 1.1 percent in 1904. Black voter registration in Alabama plummeted from 180,000 in 1900 to 3,000 in 1903. These registration figures undoubtedly overstated turnout. In Mississippi black voter turnout was estimated at 29 percent in 1888, 2 percent in 1892, and 0 percent in 1895.

When blacks could not vote, neither could they be elected to office. Sixty-four blacks had sat in the Mississippi legislature in 1873; none sat after 1895. In South Carolina's lower house, which had a black majority during Reconstruction, a single black remained in 1896. The last southern black congressman until the 1970s, George White of North Carolina, relinquished his seat in 1901.

More important, blacks could no longer be elected to local offices, such as sheriff, justice of the peace, juror, county commissioner, and school board member. In the late nineteenth century, these were the most important governmental actors. The preferred method of denying constitutional rights to blacks was to vest discretion over the administration of laws in local officials and trust them to preserve white supremacy. Disfranchisement was essential to the success of this strategy.

Southern state legislatures began to formally segregate blacks at roughly the same time that they disfranchised them. Florida enacted the first railroad segregation measure in 1887; by 1892 eight other states had followed suit. Laws segregating local streetcars swept the South between 1900 and 1906. Segregation statutes required separate-but-equal accommodations, yet in practice, segregation afforded blacks nothing like equality. "[S]carcely fit for a dog to ride in" is how one southern black described Jim Crow railroad cars.

As Congress lost interest and southern blacks lost voting rights, southern whites were able to dismantle the black education system. Most whites thought that an education spoiled good field hands, needlessly encouraged competition with white workers, and rendered blacks dissatisfied with their subordinate status.

In 1901 Georgia's governor, Allen D. Candler, stated, "God made them negroes and we cannot by education make them white folks." A few years later, the governor-elect of South Carolina, Cole

James K. Vardaman (1861–1930)

Blease, concluded, "[T]he greatest mistake the white race has ever made was in attempting to educate the free Negro." Many whites now accepted "scientific" evidence that purported to show that the black race was losing the Darwinian struggle for survival, that the race was deteriorating on the road to extinction, and that efforts to slow the decline through education were futile. Racial disparities in educational funding increased dramatically in the early years of the twentieth century.

With black political power stunted in the South, radical racists such as James Vardaman and Cole Blease swept to power. Blease bragged that he would resign as governor of South Carolina and "lead the mob," rather than use his office to protect a "nigger brute" from lynching. Governor Vardaman of Mississippi promised that "every Negro in the state will be lynched" if necessary to maintain white supremacy.

In an era of rampant lynchings, these were not empty threats. In the 1890s well over one hundred lynchings were reported annually, with some years topping two hundred. Most lynchings were of southern blacks; occasionally, the only transgression alleged was breach of racial etiquette or general "uppityness." Prosecutions of even known lynchers were rare, and convictions virtually nonexistent. Public lynchings witnessed by hundreds or thousands of spectators, many of whom brought their families and took home souvenirs from the victim's tortured body, were not uncommon.

Growing racial oppression in the South grew out of the interplay between regional developments and national ones. Economic hardship among southern farmers in the late nineteenth century fostered powerful protest movements, such as the Farmers' Alliance and the Populist Party. The growing political power of poor white farmers, whose precarious economic and social status inclined them to treasure white supremacy, did not bode well for blacks. Around the turn of the century, higher-status whites, who occasionally displayed paternalistic racial attitudes and supported qualified black rights, were supplanted by political demagogues who preached unrestrained white supremacy. The growth of Populism also impelled conservatives to invoke the threat of "Negro domination" in order to disrupt potential cross-racial alliances among poor farmers.

Yet without northern acquiescence, southern racial practices could not have become so oppressive. Several factors explain the increasing willingness of white northerners to permit white southerners a free hand in ordering southern race relations.

Black migration to the North, which more than doubled in the decades after 1890, heightened the racial anxieties of northern whites, leading to greater discrimination in public accommodations, occasional efforts to segregate public schools, and episodic outbreaks of white-on-black violence, including lynchings. Commenting on the exclusion of a black bishop from a white hotel in 1896, a black newspaper in Boston observed that "social equality appears more unthinkable today than ever." In a widely noted speech in 1907, Charles Eliot, the president of Harvard University, observed, "Perhaps if there were as many Negroes here as [in the South] we might think it better for them to be in separate schools."

The immigration of millions of southern and eastern Europeans, which began in the 1880s and accelerated around 1900, fed concern among northerners about the dilution of "Anglo-Saxon racial stock" and made them more sympathetic to southern racial policies. The resurgence of American imperialism in the 1890s, with the annexation of Hawaii and then the acquisition of Puerto Rico and the Philippines after the Spanish-American War, also fostered the convergence of northern and southern racial attitudes. Imperialists who rejected full citizenship rights for residents of the new territories were less inclined to protest the disfranchisement of blacks in the South. As one southern disfranchiser observed, territorial acquisition "has forced the race problem to the attention of the whole country and in the wise solution of this question we have the sympathy instead of the hostility of the North."

Another cause of the growing northern acquiescence to oppressive southern racial practices was the dissipation of the Republican Party's historical commitment to protecting black rights. By the 1890s three decades' worth of Republican efforts to create a viable southern wing of the party had plainly failed. After winning between 40 and 41 percent of the southern presidential vote between 1876 and 1884, the Republicans garnered only 37 percent in 1888 and 30 percent in 1896. Moreover, after the transitional elections of the mid-1890s, the Republican Party was, for the first time, able to securely maintain control of the national government without receiving significant southern electoral support, thus removing an important incentive for the protection of southern black suffrage.

For these reasons, Republican racial policy changed. In 1896 the party's national platform diluted its usual demand for a "free ballot and a fair count" in the South. After his victory that year, President McKinley declared that "the North and the South no longer divide on the old [sectional] lines." In 1899 McKinley appeared before the Georgia legislature and affirmed the national government's responsibility for the care of Confederate soldiers' graves. Republican parties in northern states ran fewer black candidates, and black representation at party conventions declined.

The Supreme Court's decisions in this era reflect these deteriorating racial conditions. In *Plessy v. Ferguson* (1896), the justices rejected a constitutional challenge to a Louisiana statute requiring railroads to provide separate and equal accommodations for black and white passengers.

The conventional sources of constitutional law supported the outcome in *Plessy*. The text of the Fourteenth Amendment does not plainly bar racial segregation. "Equal protection of the laws" seems to permit "separate but equal" facilities. The original understanding of the amendment also seemed to permit segregation, as most of its drafters and ratifiers regarded "social equality" as beyond the scope of the amendment.

Precedent clearly sustained racial segregation. In applying the common law, which required common carriers to afford access to all paying customers but allowed for "reasonable regulations" for the public's convenience, nineteenth-century courts upheld segregation as a reasonable measure that would reduce friction arising from natural "repugnancies" between the races. Federal courts interpreted the 1875 Civil Rights Act, which required that common carriers provide "full and equal" access regardless of race, to forbid both the exclusion of blacks and inferior accommodations, but not segregation. Lower courts almost unanimously construed the Fourteenth Amendment to permit racial segregation of public schools.

If precedent made the outcome in *Plessy* unsurprising, the broader racial context made it almost inevitable. By the 1890s escalating white-on-black violence in the South made racial segregation appear to be "the embodiment of enlightened public policy." An overwhelming consensus among whites favored preserving "racial purity," which counseled against permitting integrated seating on railroad cars. One leading black newspaper concluded that *Plessy* was just "another practical demonstration of the effect of public sentiment upon even the greatest judicial body in the world. We can be discriminated against, we can be robbed of our political rights, we can be persecuted and murdered and yet we cannot secure a legal redress in the courts of the United States."

The justices showed no greater solicitude for the voting rights of southern blacks. So long as southern states refrained from violating the explicit terms of the Fifteenth Amendment, the Court found a way to sustain their disfranchising practices.

Williams v. Mississippi (1898) involved a challenge to the suffrage qualifications in Mississippi's 1890 constitution. Williams argued that the requirements that voters be of "good character" and "understanding" had been adopted for a discriminatory purpose and that they conferred unbridled discretion on registrars, thus inviting discriminatory administration in violation of the Fourteenth Amendment. The justices rejected both challenges, refusing to conduct an inquiry into legislative motive and ruling that Mississippi had sufficiently constrained the discretion of administrators.

Williams had failed to demonstrate actual discrimination in the administration of voting requirements, but five years later, the justices proved equally unreceptive to such a challenge. In *Giles v. Harris* (1903), the plaintiff alleged race discrimination in the administration of Alabama's "good character and understanding" clause and sought an injunction compelling his registration.

Writing for the majority, Justice Oliver Wendell Holmes ruled that even if the allegations were proved, the plaintiff was not entitled to the requested relief. An injunction compelling his registration would be "an empty form" if Alabama whites were determined to disfranchise blacks. The plaintiff's remedy, Holmes explained, must come from the political branches of the national government.

Giles is one of the Supreme Court's most candid confessions of limited power. The decision essentially admits that hostile public opinion may prevent the redress of even plain constitutional violations. Yet one should not assume that the justices would have invalidated disfranchisement had they possessed the power to enforce such a decision. These justices were probably no more supportive of black suffrage than were most white Americans of the era.

By 1900 most white southerners were determined to eliminate black suffrage, even if doing so required violence. Southern progressives generally viewed black disfranchisement as an enlightened alternative to election fraud and violence. Many northern whites now shared the view that the Fifteenth Amendment had been a mistake and that black suffrage was a failure. Imperialist acquisitions of new territories and massive migrations from southern and eastern Europe had undermined the ideal of universal manhood suffrage.

Congress, too, reflected this shift in public opinion regarding black suffrage. In 1893–94 Democrats, enjoying simultaneous control of Congress and the presidency for the first time since before the Civil War, repealed most of the federal voting rights legislation. When Republicans regained national control from 1897 to 1911, they made no effort to reenact these laws. Moreover, Congress failed to remedy patent violations of section two of the Fourteenth Amendment, which *requires* reduction of a state's congressional representation if its adult male citizens are disfranchised for any reason other than crime. As one contemporary observed, with the Court and Congress reflecting "the apathetic tone of public opinion," the Fifteenth Amendment, though still part of the Constitution in "the technical sense," was "already in process of repeal" as "a rule of conduct."

Other Supreme Court decisions around this time made race discrimination in jury selection virtually impossible to prove, thus effectively negating earlier rulings that had barred such discrimination under the Fourteenth Amendment. The justices ruled that the lengthy absence of blacks from a county's juries raised no inference of discrimination and that criminal defendants bore the burden of overcoming the presumption that state jury commissioners had acted constitutionally in selecting jurors.

Because the Court had previously interpreted federal law to bar most jury discrimination claims from the lower federal courts, state trial judges nearly always made the initial findings on this issue. Where state courts found inadequate defendants' evidence of discrimination in jury selection, the justices deferred to those findings, thus ensuring that jury discrimination claims were evaluated only in forums that were openly committed to white supremacy. Between 1904 and 1935, the Court did not reverse the conviction of a single black defendant on the ground of race discrimination in jury selection, even though blacks were almost universally excluded from southern juries.

The justices' lack of solicitude for black jury service almost certainly reflected public opinion. By the 1890s southern whites had largely succeeded in eradicating black office holding, which included jury service. The last black—prior to the 1965 Voting Rights Act—was elected to Virginia's legislature in 1891, Mississippi's in 1895, and South Carolina's in 1902. Whites in South Carolina were so opposed to black office holding that they lynched a black U.S. postmaster in 1898.

Northern whites were not committed to protecting the ability of southern blacks to hold office. Most had never been enthusiastic about the practice, which is why the Fifteenth Amendment did not expressly protect it. Republican presidents McKinley, Roosevelt, and Taft largely ceased appointing southern blacks to federal patronage positions in order to avoid antagonizing southern whites. By 1910 blacks were no longer serving in the legislatures of most northern states, and black jury service in the North was a rare occurrence.

In 1899 the Supreme Court upheld racial inequality in public education. The school board in Richmond County, Georgia, had ceased funding the black high school, while continuing to operate a high school for whites, on the ground that the limited funds available for black education were better spent on the three hundred children in the primary schools than on the sixty in the high school. The justices rejected an equal-protection challenge to this scheme, reasoning that the board's action was not motivated by racial animus and that redistributing funds to maximize the educational opportunities of blacks as a group was reasonable. The author of the unanimous opinion was John Marshall Harlan, the only justice in *Plessy* to conclude that state-mandated segregation of railroad passengers was unconstitutional.

This result was almost certainly consonant with public opinion. By 1900 most southern whites opposed black education altogether or favored only industrial training. Public high school education was virtually nonexistent for southern blacks. In 1890 only 0.39 percent of southern black children attended high school, and in 1910 just 2.8 percent. The black public high school in Richmond County was the only one in Georgia, and one of only four in the entire South.

Northern whites, though more committed to promoting black literacy, generally agreed that southern blacks needed only a limited education. Northern philanthropic organizations, which heavily subsidized schools for southern blacks, endorsed industrial training to prepare blacks for manual labor and service positions. President McKinley, visiting the Tuskegee Institute, praised its industrial-education mission and its managers, who "evidently do not believe in attempting the unattainable." President Taft likewise observed, "I am not one of those who believe it is well to educate the mass of Negroes with academic or university education." Because the justices likely shared this predominant white view of black education, they considered it reasonable for the Richmond County school board to reallocate limited black educational funds from secondary to primary education.

Even if the Supreme Court's race rulings of this era had been more progressive, they probably would not have made much difference. Court decisions are not self-executing. Southern whites would not have voluntarily complied with judicial bans on racial segregation or black disfranchisement. The Fourteenth and Fifteenth Amendments, imposed against the will of most white southerners, exerted little moral influence upon them. Racially egalitarian judicial interpretations of those amendments would have carried no more. Only coercion by the federal government could have enforced such hypothetical rulings.

There is little reason to believe that any such coercion would have been forthcoming. Congress and the president generally reflect public opinion, which did not support racial integration, black suffrage, black jury service, or equal funding of black education. If Congress was unwilling to impose *constitutionally mandated* sanctions for disfranchisement under section two of the Fourteenth Amendment, why would it have been inclined to enforce a Court decision protecting black voting rights?

Private enforcement of civil rights rulings would likely have been no more availing. By the 1890s legal challenges by southern blacks to segregation or disfranchisement would have invited physical retaliation and perhaps even lynching. Homer Plessy could challenge segregation in the relatively tolerant racial environment of New Orleans, but probably nowhere else in the Deep South.

Even blacks inclined to litigate in defense of their rights generally would have lacked the resources necessary to do so. Most southern blacks were economically dependent on whites and thus vulnerable to economic reprisals. In any event, few white lawyers in the South would have taken such cases, and very few blacks practiced law. Until the National Association for the Advancement of Colored People (NAACP) was founded in 1909, there was no organization that could support such litigation.

Even if one could imagine blacks litigating such cases, successful lawsuits require the cooperation of local actors, such as judges and jurors. Yet by 1900 nearly all of these actors in the South were white, and none of them were likely to sympathize with blacks claiming violations of their constitutional rights. Without juries willing to convict violators and judges willing to impose significant sanctions, court decisions favorable to the rights of blacks were certain to be nullified in practice. It was for this reason that public accommodations statutes had proved notoriously ineffective.

The national government lacked sufficient administrative capacity to bypass the local enforcement apparatus. No Federal Bureau of Investigation existed, and the Justice Department lacked the resources to prosecute most civil rights violations. Few federal

funding programs existed, eliminating one potential lever for co-
ercing southern compliance with civil rights rulings. The federal
government lacked adequate personnel to commandeer the administration of elections. In short, the sort of federal bureaucratic
power that proved critical to enforcement of civil rights in the
1960s was inconceivable in 1900.

Finally, even enforceable Court decisions would have had relatively little effect on the lives of southern blacks. Most Jim Crow
laws merely symbolized white supremacy; they did not create it.
Laws played a relatively minor role in the practice of segregation.
Steamboat travel was more segregated than railroad travel, yet
only three states compelled such segregation by law. After 1900
southern courtrooms were universally segregated without statutory mandate, and segregation was pervasive in theaters, hotels,
and restaurants, even though it was rarely compelled by law.

Similarly, most southern blacks lost the vote before southern
states adopted formal disfranchisement measures. Many white
southerners admitted that disfranchisement laws were simply a
means of "purifying" the electoral system: rather than disfranchising blacks through force and fraud, legal methods would be
used to the same end. If the legal methods had been unavailable,
though, whites had proved their willingness to kill blacks in order
to secure white political supremacy. As a Kentucky newspaper
observed, "Certain it is that the white man will not again submit
to his political domination as in the days of the Carpetbagger. The
simple expedient of force will doubtless be used if all other means
fail."

An extraordinary case from Chattanooga, Tennessee, confirms that
even a greater commitment by the Supreme Court to protecting
the rights of blacks would likely have been unavailing. In 1906 a
black man, Ed Johnson, was accused of raping a white woman.

Johnson's trial, before a jury from which blacks had been systematically excluded, occurred in an atmosphere dominated by the threat of mob violence. The trial judge denied the defense's request for a continuance out of fear that delaying the trial would result in Johnson's lynching. Johnson's lawyers, who had been pressured not to vigorously cross-examine the alleged victim, did not appeal their client's conviction.

Eventually, two black lawyers intervened to petition a federal district court for a writ of habeas corpus, challenging Johnson's conviction on the grounds of race discrimination in jury selection and mob domination of the trial. The district judge denied the writ but stayed Johnson's execution pending an appeal to the U.S. Supreme Court.

Two days before the scheduled execution, the Court allowed the appeal, informing Sheriff Joseph F. Shipp of Chattanooga by telegram. The next evening, a mob, with the sheriff's connivance, broke into jail and lynched Johnson. A note was left on his mutilated body: "To Justice Harlan. Come get your nigger now."

Local officials blamed the lynching on the Supreme Court and refused to prosecute the lynchers. The Justice Department also declined to prosecute, expressing doubts about both its constitutional authority to intercede and a local jury's willingness to convict. Sheriff Shipp was reelected to office in a landslide a few days later, as his supporters warned that a vote against him would be construed as a condemnation of the lynching.

Though Shipp was ultimately convicted of criminal contempt in unprecedented proceedings before the Supreme Court, similar charges brought against most members of the lynch mob were dismissed because witnesses had been intimidated into silence. Shipp was greeted as a hero by a crowd of ten thousand when he returned home from jail.

Sheriff Joseph F. Shipp

Given the lengths to which southern whites were prepared to go in resisting federal interference with white supremacy, it is hard to see how Supreme Court decisions protecting the rights of southern blacks could have made much difference.

By 1910, according to the NAACP, courts had "touched bottom in the race problem." A black newspaper opined, "the Supreme Court has never but once decided anything in favor of the 10,000,000 Afro-Americans of this country." Given such views, blacks might easily have lost their faith in justice and the courts.

Yet disappointing Court decisions did not deter blacks from litigating. In the absence of viable alternatives, such as political protest or street demonstrations, litigation remained the most promising protest strategy available. Unlike political protest, litigation can be conducted by small numbers of people. Unlike direct-action protest, litigation was *relatively* safe, because it took place in courtrooms rather than on the streets—a significant advantage during this era of rampant white-on-black violence. So blacks continued to litigate, and from 1909 onward, they frequently had the NAACP's assistance in doing so. Victories in court lay just around the corner.

CHAPTER SIX

The Progressive Era

IN AUGUST 1906 between ten and twenty black soldiers stationed near Brownsville, Texas, allegedly went on a rampage, racing through town, firing their rifles indiscriminately, killing one white person and wounding two others. When not a single soldier in the three black companies would incriminate his comrades, President Theodore Roosevelt, at the army's behest, dishonorably discharged all 167 of the soldiers the day after the midterm congressional elections in November.

The Brownsville incident attracted national attention, including Senate hearings. Southern whites were delighted with Roosevelt's action, which drew the endorsement of several southern legislatures. Southern Democrats in Congress called for blacks to be excluded entirely from the U.S. military.

Many northern newspapers, however, condemned the president's action—going so far as to call it an "executive lynching." A group of black ministers in New England declared that Brownsville had "done more to arouse our just resentment and unite all elements of our people than any act of any President since Emancipation." One black editor wrote that "Jefferson Davis is more honored today than Theodore Roosevelt," while another observed that "the Negroes are depleting the dictionary of adjectives in their denunciation of the President."

Blacks were especially indignant that Roosevelt had endorsed the concept of group guilt in his treatment of the soldiers, which was reminiscent of his speeches blaming blacks for lynchings because of their failure to ferret out criminals in their communities. Some black leaders were so disaffected with Roosevelt that in 1908 they voted Democratic for the first time in their lives, preferring William Jennings Bryan—whom black leaders conceded was an "avowed enemy"—to their "false friends" in the Republican Party.

With the dawning of the twentieth century, racial attitudes and practices in the United States continued in a downward cycle of oppression. As black migration to the North accelerated, the migrants discovered, in the words of Senator William Borah of Idaho, that "the white man of the North is of the same race as the white man of the South, and that in his blood is the virus of dominion and power."

Many northern cities segregated their public schools for the first time in decades, and some northern colleges began segregating blacks in dormitories. Hotels, restaurants, and theaters were now more inclined to exclude blacks. Many northern states considered adopting antimiscegenation laws as a response to the marriage of Jack Johnson, the controversial black boxing champion, to a white woman.

Employment opportunities for working-class northern blacks shrank. In 1911 a black Bostonian observed, "The industrial outlook ... for the Negro is darker than since the Civil War. The blood ... of the abolitionists seems to have run out." As European immigration exploded, blacks began losing many of the jobs that had previously been available to them: barber, waiter, coachman, and chef. Increasingly powerful labor unions generally excluded blacks from membership. The use of black strikebreakers by northern industry fed the racial animosities of working-class whites.

Interracial competition for jobs and housing fostered white-on-black violence in several northern cities. In 1908 in Springfield, Illinois—Abraham Lincoln's hometown—a white mob, incensed by recent allegations of black men sexually assaulting white women, shot six blacks dead, lynched two others, and drove two thousand more out of town. When a black man was lynched in Coatesville, Pennsylvania, in 1911, a correspondent opined in the NAACP's journal, *The Crisis*, that the incident "could not have taken place, in Coatesville or elsewhere, a dozen or even half a dozen years ago." Now, however, "through the sheer power of southern example, we have come to regard a black criminal as in a different category." The president of a black college in Ohio concluded around this time: "The North has reached the point where it is ready to echo almost anything the South chooses to assert.... It thinks the early education of the Negro a mistake, the ballot a blunder, the Negro a fiend."

The situation of blacks in the South was also becoming more desperate. At the time of *Plessy*, significant numbers of blacks still voted in many southern states, but that was no longer true by 1910. As blacks stopped voting, racial disparities in educational funding became enormous, as the temptation to raid black school funds proved too great to resist. By 1915 per capita spending on white pupils was roughly three times that spent on black pupils in North Carolina, six times in Alabama, and twelve times in South Carolina.

Racial segregation was spreading into new states, such as Oklahoma and Maryland, and into new spheres of southern life.

Lynching of two black men in Marion, Indiana, in 1930

White nurses were forbidden to treat black hospital patients, and white teachers were forbidden to work in black schools. Banks established separate deposit windows for blacks. In courts, white and black witnesses were sworn in with different bibles. Southern cities adopted the first residential segregation ordinances, and a movement was afoot to segregate the southern countryside.

Economic opportunities for skilled black laborers were shrinking in the South, as whites repossessed traditionally black jobs. Black coal miners in East Tennessee lost their jobs to whites. Black lawyers increasingly found themselves out of work, as a more rigid color line forbade their presence in some courtrooms and made them liabilities to clients in others. When a strike designed to force the dismissal of black railway firemen failed, white workers simply murdered many of the blacks.

The 1912 presidential election and its aftermath revealed the hopeless situation blacks confronted in national politics. The Republican Party nominated the incumbent president, William Howard Taft, who had ordered the dismissal of the Brownsville soldiers when he was secretary of war. In his inaugural address in 1909, President Taft endorsed southern efforts to avoid domination by an "ignorant, irresponsible element," conceded that popular opinion probably no longer supported the Fifteenth Amendment, and reassured white southerners that it was not "the disposition or within the province of the Federal Government to interfere with the regulation by Southern States of their domestic affairs." Taft denied that the federal government had jurisdiction to take action against lynchings. During the 1912 campaign, he further alienated blacks by declaring that they "ought to come and [are] coming more and more under the guardianship of the South." The Republican Party platform that year abandoned even its nominal support of black voting rights.

The candidate of the newly formed Progressive Party, Theodore Roosevelt, had become anathema to many blacks. In addition to dismissing the black soldiers at Brownsville, President Roosevelt had remained silent after whites massacred blacks in Atlanta in 1906 and had blamed lynchings primarily on black rapists. He had also urged southern blacks to concentrate on moral and economic uplift, rather than politics, and had insisted that "race purity must be maintained." During the 1912 campaign, southern Progressives were openly white supremacist, and Roosevelt endorsed southern home rule on the race issue, while opposing the seating of southern black delegates at his party's national convention.

The Democratic candidate in 1912 was native Virginian Woodrow Wilson. Many blacks expressed concern about Wilson's racial views, as he had been the president of Princeton, one of the few northern colleges that completely barred blacks. But during the campaign, Wilson promised blacks justice—"not mere grudging justice, but justice executed with liberality and cordial good feeling"—though he refused to make more specific commitments on racial policy. One black editor characterized the choices facing black voters in 1912 as "three dishes of crow."

Soon after Wilson's victory, southern Cabinet members promptly segregated working, eating, and restroom facilities in their departments—a radical departure from a fifty-year tradition of an integrated civil service. The president approved this segregation as necessary to reduce interracial friction and preserve black jobs. The number of blacks holding federal civil-service positions nonetheless declined significantly, as southern senators such as James Vardaman declared war on black appointees. The great black leader W. E. B. Du Bois, who had endorsed Wilson in 1912, quickly concluded that the president had been insincere on the race question and pronounced his record one of "the most grievous disappointments that a disappointed people must bear."

The South was back in the saddle for the first time since the Civil War. Wilson was the first native southern president since Andrew Johnson, and Edward White, elevated to the position of Chief Justice by Taft, was the first native southerner to head the Court since Roger Taney. Once Democrats took control of both houses of Congress in 1913, southerners dominated congressional committees. Southern congressional representatives took advantage of their newfound control of the federal government to introduce bills to ban interracial marriage, bar blacks from becoming military officers, and repeal the Fifteenth Amendment—in effect, nationalizing southern racial policy. Though these bills had little chance of passage, they inspired some of the most racist rhetoric ever heard in Congress and forced the NAACP to divert scarce resources to opposing them.

As the plight of blacks worsened in the North and the South, anti-Japanese hysteria swept the West. Large numbers of Japanese had begun immigrating to America in the 1880s, leading nativists to complain that the Japanese were simply replacing the Chinese, who had been largely barred by the 1882 exclusion law.

The anti-Japanese movement crested in the first decade of the twentieth century, as the number of Japanese in the United States tripled, and Japan's victory in its war with Russia heightened American anxiety about Japanese imperialism. In 1905 the *San Francisco Chronicle* warned that the Japanese were "a menace to American women" and that the "raging torrent" of Japanese immigration would produce a "yellow peril." California labor unionists demanded a ban on further Japanese immigration.

In 1906 the San Francisco school board ordered the Japanese segregated into schools with the Chinese, thus creating a foreign-policy crisis. President Roosevelt privately sent his regrets to the Japanese ambassador and publicly dispatched one of his cabinet members to California to negotiate a change in policy. Roosevelt ultimately prevailed upon school board officials to change course by promising to secure self-imposed limits on Japanese immigration. These were achieved in the "Gentlemen's Agreement" of 1907–08.

A few years later President Wilson confronted a similar crisis. Expanding Japanese land ownership led the California legislature in 1913 to consider a measure barring aliens who were ineligible from citizenship—that is, Asians—from owning real estate. A crowd of twenty thousand gathered in Tokyo to demand that a naval fleet be sent to California to protect the rights of Japanese subjects. President Wilson sent Secretary of State William Jennings Bryan to California to discourage the legislature from passing the bill, but he was unsuccessful. In 1920 California voters overwhelmingly approved an even tougher measure that barred the leasing of land to Japanese nationals and prohibited noncitizens from acting as guardians for citizens in matters of land tenure, which ensured that Japanese immigrants could not use their children who had been born as U.S. citizens to circumvent the prohibition on alien ownership of land. The state of Washington passed a similar measure the following year.

Anti-Asian sentiment helped consolidate a racial alliance between the West and the South. In 1914 Senator Key Pittman of Nevada opposed the federal amendment guaranteeing women's suffrage "because he realized that its passage would embarrass the South in its treatment of the Negro problem, and ... he did not care to endanger the chances of future anti-Japanese legislation by alienating the South."

Despite such oppressive racial conditions, the Supreme Court in the 1910s vindicated several of the civil rights claims made by blacks. These decisions show that constitutional law is partly about law, not simply about politics. Even justices from whom the NAACP expected little felt bound to invalidate transparent constitutional violations.

In *Guinn v. Oklahoma* (1915), the Court ruled that the Fifteenth Amendment barred the grandfather clause—a device that insulated illiterate whites from disfranchisement by exempting from literacy tests those persons (and their descendants) who were enfranchised before 1867, when most southern blacks first received the vote. The grandfather clause was such an obvious evasion of the Fifteenth Amendment that delegates to Louisiana's 1898 constitutional convention, which was the first to adopt such a measure, warned that courts would invalidate it as a "weak and transparent subterfuge." One of the state's U.S. senators called the provision "grossly unconstitutional."

Louisiana ignored such warnings, as did several other states, which also adopted grandfather clauses. Yet all of these states but one limited the clause's duration, hoping that the purpose could be accomplished before court challenges could be filed. Only Oklahoma's grandfather clause, at issue in *Guinn*, was permanent.

Contemporary commentators regarded *Guinn* as an easy case. The *Washington Post* observed that the grandfather clause "was so obvious an evasion that the Supreme Court could not have failed to declare it unconstitutional." The *New York Times* thought "no other decision was possible" because the grandfather clause "had no reason for being unless it was for the purpose of nullifying the Fifteenth Amendment, and the court is not there to nullify the Constitution." A commentator in the *Harvard Law Review* queried, "is it not a trespass upon the dignity of a court to expect it to refuse to brush aside so thin a gauze of words?"

In 1914 the Court faced a challenge to an Oklahoma statute that permitted railroads to provide luxury accommodations, such as sleeping cars and dining cars, only to members of one race (that is, whites). In *McCabe v. Atchison, Topeka & Santa Fe Railway Co.*, the Court rejected the challenge as unripe because the statute had yet to go into operation, but five justices volunteered their view that the law violated the Equal Protection Clause. They rejected the state's defense that requiring railroads to provide equal luxury accommodations for blacks was unreasonable because per capita demand was much lower among blacks than among whites.

McCabe was a straightforward application of the dominant understanding that racially separate facilities had to be equal in order to be constitutional. In 1883 the Court had contributed to that understanding by upholding a statute punishing fornication more severely when the parties were of different races than when they were of the same race on the ground that the black party and the white party to interracial fornication were subjected to the same punishment. Lower court decisions invalidating state laws that imposed racially separate taxes for segregated schools likewise revealed an understanding that the Fourteenth Amendment permitted racial distinctions but forbade racial inequality. It was this understanding that induced every southern state adopting a railroad segregation statute to require that separate facilities be equal.

McCabe was easy politically as well as legally. The majority's dictum in no way questioned the constitutionality of segregation. Oklahoma was one of only four southern states that expressly permitted unequal luxury accommodations. These aberrational statutes illustrate the continuing deterioration in southern race relations: segregation was no longer sufficient for white southerners; they now demanded formal inequality as well. *McCabe* simply held a few renegades to the norm accepted by all southern states a decade earlier and still adhered to by most.

In 1917 the Court faced a challenge to a residential segregation ordinance adopted in Louisville, Kentucky. The law provided that houses sold on majority-white blocks could be occupied only by whites and those sold on majority-black blocks could be occupied only by blacks.

As rural blacks flocked to cities in search of better economic opportunities, education, and physical security, black neighborhoods became congested. Middle-class blacks often sought to escape crime, vice, and grossly substandard housing by moving into white neighborhoods. Whites responded by pressuring city councils to enact residential segregation ordinances, which were defended as necessary to preserve social peace, protect racial purity, and safeguard property values. Beginning in 1910 many southern cities passed such ordinances. In *Buchanan v. Warley*, the Court invalidated them under the Fourteenth Amendment.

Buchanan was not as legally straightforward as *Guinn* and *McCabe*. If state-mandated segregation was permissible in contexts such as railroad seating, as *Plessy* had determined, why not in housing? Indeed, one could argue that segregation in housing was a more defensible exercise of the state's police power to protect health, safety, and morals, because interracial contact in housing was less transient—and therefore more threatening—than on railroads.

Although *Buchanan* may have represented a departure from *Plessy*, the outcome was more attributable to the justices' commitment to property rights than to their racial egalitarianism. *Buchanan* was decided at a time when the Court's defense of property rights was near its zenith. Indeed, in order to distinguish *Buchanan* from *Plessy*, the NAACP argued the case principally in property-rights terms.

The Court's most notorious racist, James C. McReynolds, joined the unanimous opinion in *Buchanan*—confirming that concerns about property rights drove the decision. Furthermore, three of the five southern courts that had considered the issue prior to *Buchanan* had invalidated residential segregation ordinances, emphasizing the "inalienable right to own, acquire, and dispose of property." By contrast, southern judges had no qualms about sustaining segregation in public schools or on common carriers.

Public opinion outside of the South may well have supported *Buchanan*. Charles Bonaparte, a former attorney general of the United States, ridiculed residential segregation ordinances as "petty, impolitic, medieval in conception, injurious to the best interests of the city, worthy, perhaps, of Russia." The *New York Evening Post* thought it "utterly absurd in this day and generation to return to the ghetto of the middle ages, abandoned by Europe long ago." The *Nation* praised *Buchanan* for holding "that the most hateful institution of the Russia which has passed away shall not be set up under the American flag."

None of the Court's Progressive-era race rulings made much practical difference. *Guinn*'s implications for black suffrage were trivial. By 1915 the grandfather clauses of every state but Oklahoma had already achieved their purpose and been extinguished by sunset provisions. Moreover, the Court in *Guinn* explicitly noted that a literacy test uncorrupted by a grandfather clause was permissible. The experiences of Mississippi and South Carolina, disfranchisement pioneers, already had demonstrated that a literacy test without a grandfather clause could nullify black suffrage, so long as it was administered by registrars committed to white supremacy.

Guinn also had no effect on other disfranchisement techniques, such as poll taxes, white primaries, complex registration requirements, fraud, and violence. For this reason, a New Orleans newspaper confidently concluded that *Guinn* was "not of the slightest political importance in the South." One northern newspaper predicted that blacks would discover that "getting the right to vote from the Supreme Court in Washington is not exactly the same thing as getting the right from the election board in their own voting district." The *New York Times* assured readers, "The white man will rule his land. The only question left by the Supreme Court's decision is how he will rule it."

Even in Oklahoma, *Guinn* had no effect on black voter registration, as the legislature responded to the decision by immediately "grandfathering" the grandfather clause. Under the new statute, voters in the 1914 congressional election, when the grandfather clause was still in effect, were automatically registered. All other eligible voters, including essentially all blacks, had to register within a two-week period or be forever disfranchised.

The federal government failed to challenge this patent evasion of *Guinn*, and the justices had no opportunity to invalidate it until 1939. At a time when the NAACP's annual legal budget was roughly five thousand dollars, and it had fewer than fifteen local branches—almost all of them in the North—follow-up litigation was hard to come by. Yet without it, judicial rulings protecting civil rights were easily nullified in practice.

McCabe almost certainly had no effect on the railroad accommodations of southern blacks. The Constitution, as interpreted by the Court, required only that state *law* not authorize inequality. Actual conditions for railway passengers were governed not by the Constitution but by the common law of common carriers, state statutes providing for separate-but-equal facilities, and the Interstate Commerce Act's prohibition on "undue or unreasonable prejudice or disadvantage."

Common-law challenges to racially unequal railroad accommodations had frequently succeeded through the mid-1880s, but such cases virtually disappeared thereafter. Similarly, the Interstate Commerce Commission (ICC) had challenged racial discrimination on railroads in the late 1880s, but by the Progressive era, the ICC was largely deferring to southern railroads' denials of discrimination. Suspecting inhospitable forums, black litigants rarely, if ever, challenged racial inequalities in railroad accommodations under state separate-but-equal statutes. Thus, so long as state legislatures refrained from codifying inequality, *McCabe* left railroads free to treat black passengers as they pleased.

Unfettered by meaningful legal constraints, southern railroads provided black passengers with accommodations that were anything but equal. Conditions in Jim Crow cars were vile; the NAACP described them as "a nightmare of discomfort, insecurity and insult." Black cars were "stifling with the odor of decayed fruit," seats were filthy, and the air was "fetid." White passengers entered at will to smoke, drink, and antagonize blacks. Convicts and the insane were relegated to these cars. Such conditions plainly violated state law—and with regard to interstate travel, they violated federal law as well—yet they prevailed throughout the South, and generally without prompting legal challenges.

Buchanan had no effect on segregated housing patterns. In most of the South, legal regulation was unnecessary to maintain residential segregation because, as one southern newspaper explained, "There may be no written law saying where a Negro shall live and where a white man shall live, but in a white man's town there need be no law." Even in northern cities such as Chicago and New York, where residential segregation ordinances were never seriously contemplated, residential segregation dramatically increased in the 1910s and 1920s, as a result of the Great Migration of blacks to the North.

Many alternative methods of maintaining residential segregation remained available after *Buchanan*. Racially restrictive covenants in housing contracts quickly emerged as substitutes for segregation ordinances, and virtually every court decision until 1948 rejected constitutional challenges to their judicial enforcement. Agreements among real-estate agents also prevented blacks from entering white neighborhoods. City-planning officials surreptitiously zoned by race, undeterred by *Buchanan*. Public officials strategically located schools, highways, and public housing to maintain segregation. Banks would rarely lend to blacks seeking admission to white neighborhoods, and discriminatory underwriting policies of the federal government also entrenched housing segregation.

Working-class whites, more threatened by black competition for jobs and more dependent on home investments, simply used force to exclude blacks. Black families entering white neighborhoods frequently faced harassment, bombings, and mob violence. Between 1917 and 1921, Chicago had fifty-eight such bombings. White police forces almost never protected black "intruders" or even investigated such attacks. Blacks who defended themselves from mob assaults frequently faced arrest and prosecution.

Even if Progressive-era race rulings had little direct impact, they may have mattered in other ways. Success for any social-protest movement requires convincing potential participants that its goals are feasible. Especially during an era when racial oppression must have seemed immutable, civil rights victories in court may have helped keep hope alive for blacks.

Thus, Oswald Garrison Villard, the grandson of the great abolitionist William Lloyd Garrison, observed that *Buchanan* was "the most hopeful thing that has happened for some time in this dark period of our country's history." Booker T. Washington, while conceding that *Guinn* would make no "great difference in the South," thought that "[t]he moral influence of any ... court decision that guarantees freedom must awaken confidence where [it has] been lacking."

Furthermore, regardless of whether lawsuits produced victories in court, they may have been an important form of racial protest. One precondition for eventually overthrowing white supremacy was empowering southern blacks to overcome the norms of deference and subordination that many had internalized in self-defense. Racial change could not occur without southern blacks fighting for it.

Protest had to start somewhere, yet the southern caste system insulated itself from challenges from within. Political protest was unavailable, given black disfranchisement. Economic protest was difficult when blacks had so few resources. Social protest in the form of street demonstrations would likely have incited deadly retaliation at a time when blacks were frequently lynched for less. In such an oppressive environment, litigation may have been the only protest option realistically available.

At a time when white southerners could freely segregate, disfranchise, and lynch blacks, the Court proved a barrier to schemes that came too close to formal nullification of the Constitution. Yet because the justices challenged only the form, not the substance, of southern racial practices, nothing significant changed for blacks.

The justices eventually discovered that they could make a dent in Jim Crow only by penetrating form to reach substance. Decades later they began investigating legislatures' motives, questioning the fact findings of southern trial courts, eviscerating the line between public and private discrimination, and generally questioning the good faith of southern whites.

Progressive-era justices had no inclination for such undertakings, which public opinion would not have supported anyway. A Congress that would not even consider antilynching legislation and a president who pioneered segregation of the federal civil service were not about to enlist in a judicial crusade against Jim Crow. With race relations reaching a post–Civil War nadir, minimalist and inconsequential Court rulings on race were about the most that could have been expected.

CHAPTER SEVEN

Between the World Wars

IN 1919 BLACK tenant farmers and sharecroppers in Phillips County, Arkansas, tried to organize a union and to hire white lawyers to sue planters for holding them in peonage. The local whites responded by shooting their way into a church where black unionists were meeting. The unionists returned the gunfire, a white man was killed, and mayhem quickly ensued. Supported by federal troops, who had ostensibly been dispatched to quell the disturbance, marauding whites went on a rampage, tracking blacks throughout the countryside and killing dozens.

Seventy-nine blacks—but not a single white—were prosecuted and convicted for their actions during this "race riot." Twelve received the death penalty. Each trial lasted only an hour or two, and all-white juries deliberated for only a few minutes before convicting. Huge mobs of angry whites surrounded the courthouse, menacing the defendants and the jurors and threatening a lynching. Six of the defendants appealed their death sentences to

The Phillips County defendants, photographed at the Arkansas State Penitentiary

the U.S. Supreme Court, where they won a ruling that mob-dominated trials deny due process of law.

The Phillips County racial massacre illustrates both the heightened militancy that World War I inspired among blacks and the ruthless determination of southern whites to suppress it. The Court's willingness to save the defendants from execution suggests that the war also influenced the justices' views on race.

Racial attitudes and practices, which had been deteriorating since the end of Reconstruction, finally started to become more progressive in the years following World War I. One important cause of this shift was the northward migration of southern blacks, which exploded during the war, as industrial labor shortages created unprecedented job opportunities for blacks. A half million southern blacks migrated north in the 1910s, and another million in the 1920s. Between 1910 and 1930, Chicago's black population increased from 44,000 to 233,000, and Detroit's black population grew from 5,700 to 120,000.

As blacks relocated from a region of pervasive disfranchisement to one that extended suffrage without racial restriction, their
political power grew. At the local level, northern blacks began
securing the appointment of black police officers, the creation of
playgrounds and parks for black neighborhoods, and the election
of black city council members and state legislators. Not long
thereafter, northern blacks began influencing national politics—
successfully pressuring both the House of Representatives to pass
an antilynching bill in 1922 and the Senate to defeat the Supreme
Court nomination of John Parker, a southern federal judge who
had previously defended white political supremacy, in 1930.

Blacks moved North primarily in search of better job opportunities, but their rising economic status also facilitated social
protest. Larger black populations in northern cities provided a
broader economic base for black entrepreneurs and professionals,
such as teachers, ministers, lawyers, and doctors—groups which
would later supply resources and leadership for civil rights protests. Improved economic status also enabled blacks to use boycotts as levers for social change, beginning with the "don't shop
where you can't work" campaigns of the 1930s.

Northern blacks received better education, which also facilitated subsequent social protest. The more flexible racial mores of
the North permitted challenges to the status quo that would not
have been tolerated in the South. Protest organizations, such as
the NAACP, and militant black newspapers, such as the *Chicago
Defender*, developed and thrived. Because of a less rigid caste
structure, blacks in the North were less likely to internalize racist
norms of black subordination and inferiority, which posed major
obstacles to creating a racial protest movement in the South.

Before the northern migration, southern blacks moved from
farms to cities within the South. Better economic opportunities in
cities eventually fostered a black middle class, which capitalized

on the segregated economy to develop sufficient wealth and leisure time to participate in social protest. Many blacks in the urban South were economically independent of whites and thus could challenge the racial status quo without endangering their livelihoods.

Blacks in the urban South also found better education and, occasionally, freer access to the ballot box. Because racial etiquette in cities was somewhat less oppressive than in the countryside, urban blacks were more able to participate in social protest. Finally, because urban blacks lived closer to one another, enjoyed better communication and transportation facilities, and shared social networks through black colleges and churches, they found it somewhat easier to overcome the organizational obstacles confronting any social protest movement.

World War I had more immediate implications for race relations, including the ideological ramifications of a "war to make the world safe for democracy." In 1919 W. E. B. Du Bois of the NAACP wrote: "Make way for Democracy! We saved it in France, and by the Great Jehovah, we will save it in the United States of America, or know the reason why."

The war inspired blacks, who had borne arms for their country and faced death on the battlefield, to assert their rights. A black journalist noted, "The men who did not fear the trained veterans of Germany will hardly run from the lawless Ku Klux Klan." Returning black soldiers were treated as heroes in the black community, spoke to NAACP branches about their experiences, and demanded voting rights. Membership in the NAACP skyrocketed from 10,000 in 1917 to 91,000 in 1919.

While deep-rooted forces such as urbanization and the Great Migration would eventually facilitate the development of a civil rights movement, the immediate prospects for African Americans in 1920 were bleak. The migration of southern blacks to the North fed the racial prejudice of northern whites, who used racially re-strictive covenants, hostile neighborhood associations, and vio-lence to keep blacks from moving into their neighborhoods. Housing segregation increased dramatically in the 1920s and translated directly into increased segregation in schools. The in-flux of *white* southerners to northern cities further exacerbated racial tensions and led to enormous increases in Ku Klux Klan membership: by the mid-1920s, there were an estimated 35,000 Klansmen in Detroit and 50,000 in Chicago.

Blacks who remained in the South faced even worse prospects. Many southern counties with large black populations did not provide high schools for blacks until the 1930s. With regard to parks, playgrounds, and beaches, "separate but equal" frequently meant that blacks got nothing.

Fearful that returning black soldiers would launch a social revolution, southern whites prepared for a race war. Black soldiers were assaulted, forced to shed their uniforms, and sometimes lynched. In 1919, when the NAACP's national secretary, John Shillady, traveled to Austin, Texas, to defend a beleaguered branch from state legal harassment, three white men beat him nearly into unconsciousness in broad daylight—without legal repercussion. In 1920 in Orange County, Florida, thirty blacks were burned to death after one black man attempted to vote.

The national government offered little hope to blacks. The racial policies of the Harding, Coolidge, and Hoover administra-tions were abysmal. In 1924 Congress drastically restricted the immigration of southern and eastern Europeans who were deemed to be of inferior "racial stock"—mostly Italian Catholics and Polish and Russian Jews—and forbade all Asian immigration. After southern Democrats in the Senate in 1922 successfully fili-bustered the antilynching bill passed by the House, Republicans dropped the measure for the remainder of the decade. Republican administrations did not curtail segregation and discrimination in the federal civil service; they did not appoint blacks to patronage positions; and they did not support black factions in struggles for control of southern Republican parties. In the mid-1920s, the NAACP told its followers that Republican presidents were no better than Democratic ones, "and Democratic presidents are little better than nothing."

By the 1930s the Great Depression had left blacks in a desperately poor economic condition, and race discrimination pervaded government relief programs. Yet President Franklin D. Roosevelt's New Deal ultimately proved to be a turning point in American race relations. Its objective was helping poor people— and blacks, as the poorest of the poor, benefited disproportionately. After decades of malign neglect from the federal government, the New Deal raised the hopes and expectations of blacks. President Roosevelt also appointed a "black cabinet" of advisers within government departments. Eleanor Roosevelt served as an intermediary between black leaders and the administration, and she wrote newspaper columns criticizing race discrimination.

Roosevelt quickly became the most admired president among blacks since Abraham Lincoln. With the popularity of the New Deal making some northern states politically competitive for the first time in generations, and blacks no longer dependably voting Republican, both parties had renewed incentives to appeal for black votes. An unprecedented thirty black delegates attended the Democratic national convention in 1936; a black minister gave the invocation; and a black congressman from Chicago gave the welcoming address.

By the late 1930s racial attitudes and practices in the South were becoming slightly more progressive. Black voter registration nudged upwards, and in a few cities, blacks ran for local office for the first time in generations. Defunct branches of the NAACP were revived. Racial disparities in educational funding slowly narrowed outside of the Deep South. Opinion polls revealed that the majority of white southerners for the first time supported federal antilynching legislation.

Incipient racial progress also occurred in the North. The New Deal inspired record numbers of northern blacks to register to vote. This increased political power resulted in more black officeholders and stronger state public accommodations laws. Some northern churches began criticizing racial segregation, and some Catholic schools started admitting blacks.

By 1940 blacks had greater reason for optimism than at any time since Reconstruction. However, the actual changes in racial policies had been minor. President Roosevelt continued to oppose civil rights bills, and the antilynching measure still could not survive Senate filibuster. The disfranchisement of southern blacks remained nearly universal outside of the largest cities, and segregation remained deeply entrenched in the South and was spreading in the neighborhoods and schools of the North.

The Supreme Court's interwar racial jurisprudence reflected these slowly changing social and political conditions. The most striking victories for civil rights came in four criminal cases that revealed southern Jim Crow at its worst. *Moore v. Dempsey* (1923), the case arising from the 1919 racial massacre in Phillips County, Arkansas, reversed the death sentences of six blacks on the ground that trials dominated by the influence of a lynch mob deny due process of law.

Two other decisions, *Powell v. Alabama* (1932) and *Norris v. Alabama* (1935), involved the infamous trials of the Scottsboro Boys. Nine teenaged black youths, who were impoverished, illiterate, and transient, were charged with raping two white women on a freight train in northern Alabama in 1931. They were tried

The Scottsboro Boys

in a mob-dominated atmosphere, and eight of the nine received death sentences. The Supreme Court twice reversed their convictions—the first time because their lawyers had been appointed on the morning of the trial and the second time because of race discrimination in jury selection.

The last of these rulings, *Brown v. Mississippi* (1936), reversed the death sentences of three black sharecroppers convicted of murdering their white landlord. The confessions of the defendants, which constituted the principal evidence of their guilt, had been extracted through torture. The Court ruled that convictions based on such evidence deny due process.

These four cases arose from three similar episodes. Southern blacks were charged with serious crimes against whites—rape or murder. Mobs consisting of thousands of whites surrounded the courthouses and demanded that the defendants be turned over for execution, and lynchings were barely avoided. The defendants' guilt was in serious doubt, and several of them had been tortured into confessing. Defense lawyers were appointed no more than a day before the trials, which lasted no more than a few hours. Juries, from which blacks were intentionally excluded, deliberated only a few minutes before imposing death sentences.

Not one of these defendants was plainly guilty; it is possible that all of them were innocent. Yet guilt or innocence was often beside the point when southern blacks were accused of killing white men or sexually assaulting white women. Rejecting the NAACP's request that he represent the Scottsboro defendants on appeal, an Alabama congressional representative explained, "I don't care whether they are innocent or guilty. They were found riding on the same freight car with two white women, and that's enough for me!"

Before World War I, these defendants would likely have been lynched. By the interwar period, however, the annual number of lynchings had declined dramatically. One particularly important reason for the decline was the ability of southern states to replace lynchings with quick trials that dependably produced guilty verdicts, death sentences, and swift executions. Prosecutors in such cases often urged juries to convict in order to reward mobs for their good behavior, and governors justified refusing to commute death sentences on the same basis.

These state-imposed death sentences were little more than a formalization of the lynching process. Such farcical proceedings invited intervention by Supreme Court justices who believed that criminal trials were supposed to determine guilt, not merely prevent lynchings. Had the injustices been less obvious, the Court might have been reluctant to intervene. Yet even justices who showed little solicitude for the interests of blacks were offended by these "legal lynchings."

The Court also considered several constitutional challenges to "white primaries" during this period. Because the Democratic Party dominated southern politics after the 1890s, excluding blacks from the party's primaries effectively nullified their political influence. In *Nixon v. Herndon* (1927), the Court invalidated a Texas statute that barred blacks from participating in primary elections. The ruling was of limited significance, however, because Texas was the only state that excluded blacks from primaries by statute.

After *Herndon*, the Texas legislature immediately passed a law that empowered party executive committees to prescribe membership qualifications, and the Democratic Party executive then passed a resolution excluding blacks. Because the Constitution restricts only discriminatory *state* action, and political parties purport to be *private* organizations, the Texas Democratic Party argued that its rule excluding blacks was permissible. By a five-to-four vote, the justices in *Nixon v. Condon* (1932) disagreed, ruling that the state was constitutionally responsible for the exclusion of blacks because the Texas legislature—not the state Democratic Party—had empowered the party's executive committee to prescribe membership qualifications.

Condon only deferred the more fundamental state-action question: Did the Constitution permit a political party to bar blacks from membership? Three weeks after *Condon*, the annual convention of the Texas Democratic Party voted to exclude blacks. In *Grovey v. Townsend* (1935), the Court unanimously rejected a Fourteenth Amendment challenge to this racial exclusion on the ground that no state action was present, emphasizing that Texas neither paid for primary elections nor counted the ballots. But the Court failed to explain why these instances of state inaction counted for more than Texas's numerous actions in regulating party primaries: requiring that they be held, that voter qualifications be the same as in general elections, that absentee voting be permitted, and that election judges enjoy certain powers.

Thus, without any hint of dissent, the Supreme Court ruled that the Constitution permitted blacks to be barred from the only southern elections that mattered.

This Court also failed to strike down "private" actions that produced housing segregation. In *Corrigan v. Buckley* (1926), the Court unanimously rejected a constitutional challenge to contractual agreements not to sell real estate to blacks. The justices dismissed as frivolous the claim that the private covenants were themselves state action. In dicta, the Court announced that even *judicial enforcement* of such covenants would not qualify as state action in violation of the Fourteenth Amendment.

Judicial precedent strongly supported this result, as did the broader racial context of the 1920s. The Great Migration transformed residential segregation from a southern issue into a national one. Northern blacks seeking to purchase homes in white neighborhoods endured bombings, cross burnings, and mob assaults. In 1925 the NAACP's annual report described "segregation by terrorism" in the North. A black newspaper observed that while lynching was the South's peculiar institution, residential segregation was quickly becoming that of the North.

In the summer of 1924, huge mobs of angry whites violently repulsed the efforts of five different blacks to buy homes in white neighborhoods in Detroit. Ten thousand Klansmen gathered to burn a cross and demand a residential segregation ordinance. Police officers made little or no effort to defend the black families. When blacks who were inside the home of Dr. Ossian Sweet defended themselves, all eleven of them were charged with murder for the death of a white man who had been killed by shots fired from within the house.

The NAACP sought to convince the public that its legal challenges to racially restrictive covenants and its defense of Dr. Sweet from murder charges were facets of a common strategy to challenge residential segregation. But many whites drew a lesson different from the one intended by the NAACP: if northern whites violently resisted residential integration, then peaceful means of segregating neighborhoods, such as restrictive covenants, should be encouraged. Even many whites who were generally sympathetic to the plight of blacks felt that "any colored person who endangers life and property, simply to gratify his personal pride, is an enemy of his race as well as an incitant [sic] of riot and murder."

By the 1930s the Federal Housing Agency's underwriting manual explicitly promoted racially restrictive covenants. Federal agencies selected public housing projects with an eye toward preserving segregated housing patterns. With the national government encouraging restrictive covenants and residential segregation, it is unsurprising that the Supreme Court would interpret the Constitution to permit such arrangements.

In *Gong Lum v. Rice* (1927), the justices unanimously rejected a Chinese American's challenge to Mississippi's decision to send her to a black school rather than a white one. Misconceiving the lawsuit as an attack on racial segregation in public education, Chief Justice William Howard Taft observed that lower court precedent had conclusively sustained the constitutionality of that practice.

By 1927 schools in many northern cities were growing more segregated, as a result of growing black populations, increasing residential segregation, and hardening racial attitudes among whites. Northern blacks were divided over whether to challenge such segregation, which usually ensured jobs for black teachers and enabled black students to avoid the hostility and insults that they would endure in integrated schools. The NAACP's W. E. B. Du Bois argued that it was "idiotic simply to sit on the side lines and yell: 'No segregation' in an increasingly segregated world." Blacks were being "crucified" in integrated schools, and it was "suicidal" for them to concede the inferiority of their own schools by demanding integration.

Southern blacks knew better than to challenge an aspect of Jim Crow that was so dear to whites. The policy of the NAACP at this time was to contest the spread of school segregation in the North but not in the South, where it was so entrenched that a legal challenge would have been fruitless and possibly suicidal. Because Gong Lum did not directly challenge segregation and because Mississippi Chinese were not blacks, a respected local law firm took the case, and the trial judge granted relief without outraging local opinion. Had blacks challenged school segregation in Mississippi at this time, the reaction would have been very different.

In 1938 Lloyd Gaines, a black man, challenged Missouri's policy of providing out-of-state tuition grants to blacks who sought graduate and professional education, which was denied to them in Missouri. Judicial precedent had long established that racially segregated public facilities had to be equal to be constitutional. The Supreme Court now ruled that shipping blacks out of state for higher education did not satisfy that requirement.

By 1938, with black professionals playing unprecedented roles in federal administrative agencies, the justices may have found the wholesale exclusion of blacks from higher education in the South incongruous. Strikingly, *Gaines* was argued by a black lawyer, Charles Hamilton Houston, who epitomized through his Harvard legal pedigree and his exemplary forensic skills what blacks could achieve if afforded equal educational opportunities. Moreover, the justices were becoming more solicitous of the interests of racial and religious minorities. The same year as *Gaines*, Justice Harlan

Lloyd Gaines (1913–??)

Fiske Stone wrote to a friend, "I have been deeply concerned about the increasing racial and religious intolerance which seems to bedevil the world, and which I greatly fear may be augmented in this country."

The immediate consequences of this era's pro-civil-rights rulings were minimal. After *Powell v. Alabama* ruled that the appointment of counsel on the morning of trial was constitutionally inadequate, southern judges began appointing lawyers a few days before trial. Black defendants whose lives were in jeopardy were routinely provided lawyers so near to trial that no serious investigation of facts or preparation of trial strategy was possible.

Norris v. Alabama had a similarly negligible effect on black representation on southern juries. In states where jury service was tied to voter registration, *Norris* made no difference at all, as blacks remained almost universally disfranchised. In other states, *Norris* still permitted the use of typical jury selection methods that vested enormous discretion in jury commissioners. Proving race discrimination in the administration of such schemes was extremely difficult because state court judges, who were unsympathetic toward black jury service, made the initial factual determinations.

In a case reaching the Court in 1939, a rural parish in Louisiana where the population was nearly 50 percent black "complied" with *Norris* by placing three blacks, one of whom was dead, on the panel of three hundred people from which juries were selected. Furthermore, the few blacks who were called to serve on juries could usually be intimidated. When a black college president in Texas refused to be excused from jury service in 1938, white hoodlums removed him from the jury room and threw him head first down the steps of a Dallas courthouse.

Gaines too had little effect. Only Maryland and West Virginia integrated any institutions of higher education, and a few other

border states began providing rudimentary graduate and professional education for blacks in segregated schools. Astonishingly,
most southern states responded to *Gaines* by adopting the same
out-of-state scholarship laws that the Court had invalidated. Five
states had such laws before *Gaines*—by 1943 eleven did, with six
more following suit by 1948. These laws were an improvement
over what had previously been offered to blacks—nothing—but
they were in blatant disregard of *Gaines*.

Litigation in defense of the rights of southern blacks may have
been more important for its intangible effects: convincing blacks
that the racial status quo was malleable, instructing them about
their rights, helping to mobilize protest, and educating northern
whites about Jim Crow conditions. The NAACP's national office
wrote letters to southern blacks explaining their rights; some
black communities in the South felt so hopeless and isolated that
for the national office merely to make inquiries on their behalf
was empowering. A memorandum by Charles Houston declared
that a principal objective of litigation should be "to arouse and
strengthen the will of local communities to demand and fight for
their rights."

Houston and Thurgood Marshall, who took over as the
NAACP's chief litigator in the late 1930s, believed that organizing
local communities in support of litigation was nearly as important
as winning lawsuits. Because of the need "to back up our legal
efforts with the required public support and social force," Houston referred to himself as "not only lawyer but evangelist and
stump speaker." Cases such as Scottsboro demonstrated to blacks
the importance of joining together in self-defense, and thus provided unparalleled fund-raising and branch-building opportunities for the NAACP. As one black editorialist observed, "Whatever
else happens in the Scottsboro case,...[i]t has given us one of

the greatest chances for consolidated action we have had since emancipation."

Litigation also provided southern black communities with salutary examples of the skill and courage of African Americans. Watching a talented black lawyer subject a white witness to a grueling cross-examination educated and inspired southern blacks, who virtually never witnessed scenes of blacks confronting whites on an equal footing. Bold and capable performances by black lawyers in southern courtrooms seemed to contravene the very premises of white supremacy.

Marshall explained this dynamic in connection with a 1941 criminal trial in Hugo, Oklahoma, a town where no black lawyer had ever appeared in the courtroom. Marshall and his white co-counsel had agreed that Marshall would cross-examine all of the police officers, "because we figured they would resent being questioned by a Negro and would get angry and this would help us. It worked perfect. They all became angry at the idea of a Negro pushing them into tight corners and making their lies so obvious." Marshall continued: "Boy, did I like that—and did the Negroes in the Court-room like it. You can't imagine what it means to those people down there who have been pushed around for years to know that there is an organization that will help them. They are really ready to do their part now. They are ready for anything."

Litigation may also have raised the salience of racial issues for whites. As black leader Ralph Bunche noted, "Court decisions, favorable or unfavorable, serve to dramatize the plight of the race more effectively than any other recourse; their propaganda and educative value is great." Criminal cases may have afforded the best educational opportunities, as they revealed Jim Crow at its worst—southern blacks, possibly innocent of the crimes charged, being railroaded to the death penalty through farcical trials. As one black newspaper observed, "No single event touching the

Negro question in this country has been forced into the conscience, the life and the public opinion of the American people as has the Scottsboro case."

Finally, litigation, when successful, provided blacks with one of their few reasons for optimism before World War II. As one black leader observed in 1935, even if court victories produced little concrete change, they could at least "keep open the door of hope to the Negro." Roscoe Dunjee, the NAACP's principal agent in Oklahoma, noted after one such litigation triumph, "It is just such rifts in the dark clouds of prejudice which cause black folks to know that a better day is coming by and by."

By the late 1930s, the NAACP was detecting "a new South ... in the making." Several thousand blacks had recently registered to vote in large southern cities, racial disparities in educational funding were starting to decline, and southern branches of the NAACP were showing new signs of life. While significant, such changes must be kept in perspective. In 1940 southern Democrats in the Senate could still filibuster to death any civil rights bill, and southern blacks were as segregated as ever. Racial change appeared to be in the offing, but it was the cataclysmic events surrounding World War II, not the Great Depression or the New Deal, that sparked a revolution in American racial attitudes and practices.

· · ·

CHAPTER EIGHT

World War II

ETOY FLETCHER, a black veteran of World War II, tried to register to vote in rural Mississippi in 1946. The white registrar informed him, "Niggers are not allowed to vote in Rankin County, and if you don't want to get into serious trouble get out of this building and don't mention voting any more." While waiting for a bus out of town, Fletcher was kidnapped by four whites who drove him into the woods, beat him mercilessly, and warned him that he would be killed if he ever again attempted to vote.

Many other aspiring black voters reported similar experiences in Mississippi that summer. Theodore Bilbo, a U.S. senator from Mississippi running for reelection, exhorted every "red blooded white man to use any means to keep the Niggers away from the polls." While not explicitly advocating violence, Bilbo slyly observed that "[y]ou and I know what's the best way to keep the nigger from voting. You do it the night before the election. I don't have to tell you any more than that. Red-blooded men know what I mean."

Throughout Mississippi, enthusiastic supporters took the senator at his word. The *Jackson Daily News* warned blacks who were contemplating voting, "DON'T TRY IT," or else risk "unhealthy and unhappy results." Whites burned crosses in Jackson. In Biloxi, a street sign warned blacks to "vote at your own risk." In Pucket, four whites beat and threatened to kill a black man for attempting to register.

Yet Bilbo's thinly veiled exhortations of violence backfired. While Mississippi whites in the past had threatened and beaten black voters without serious repercussions, circumstances had changed by 1946. A white man from Oklahoma informed Bilbo that his speech was reminiscent of the sentiments of that "late departed and unlamented jerk in Germany," and he admonished the senator that "the time for this narrow-minded race hatred stuff is out." Labor leader Sidney Hillman sent a telegram to President Harry S. Truman to protest "the mad rantings of Senator Bilbo" who had "virtually appealed for mob action to prevent voting by Negroes."

Bilbo had unwittingly challenged the federal government to prove that it could enforce the voting rights of southern blacks. The Justice Department began an investigation of Fletcher's case, and the Senate convened hearings into Bilbo's reelection campaign. Roughly 150 Mississippi blacks—many of them war veterans and some displaying their good-conduct medals—testified at committee hearings in Jackson about the violence they had endured while attempting to vote. The *New York Times* observed that the hearings "certainly gave the rest of the country a liberal education in what white supremacy and one-party rule really mean." The *Washington Post* declared it impossible to read the committee's report without "a sense of sickness" at the brutality. The number of blacks registered to vote in Mississippi rose by 50 percent in the year following the hearings.

Had it not been for the Second World War, Etoy Fletcher probably would not have tried to vote in Mississippi in 1946, nor would the federal government have intervened on his behalf. World War II was a watershed in the history of American race relations.

The ideology of the Second World War was antifascist and pro-democratic. President Franklin D. Roosevelt urged Americans to "refut[e] at home the very theories which we are fighting abroad." Secretary of the Navy Frank Knox declared, "An army fighting allegedly for democracy should be the last place in which to practice undemocratic segregation."

Most blacks readily perceived the bitter irony in America's fighting against world fascism with a racially segregated army, and they were determined to battle injustice at home as well as abroad. The *Pittsburgh Courier,* a leading black newspaper, observed, "[O]ur war is not against Hitler in Europe, but against the Hitlers in America." In 1944 black college students seeking to desegregate a restaurant in the District of Columbia carried signs asking, "Are you for Hitler's way or the American way?"

Enemy propagandists supplied more concrete incentives for Americans to reconsider their racial practices. Within forty-eight hours of the lynching of Cleo Wright—a black man—in Sikeston, Missouri, in 1942, Axis radio broadcast the details of his murder around the world. For the first time in American history, the federal government now claimed authority over lynchings because of their international significance.

During the war blacks began to demand their citizenship rights more forcefully. James Hinton, an NAACP leader in South Carolina, reported that blacks were "aroused as never before, and we expect great things to come from this awakening." Roughly four hundred thousand blacks joined the NAACP during the war.

Southern blacks registered to vote in record numbers and demanded admission to Democratic Party primaries. Weary of Jim Crow indignities, many southern blacks refused to be segregated any longer on streetcars and buses, standing their ground when challenged and provoking almost daily racial altercations.

World War II afforded unprecedented political opportunities for blacks to leverage concessions from the Roosevelt administration. A. Philip Randolph, the head of the Brotherhood of Sleeping Car Porters, sponsored the March on Washington Movement, which sought to mobilize one hundred thousand blacks to march on the nation's capital in 1941 to protest race discrimination in the military and in defense industries. The prospect of such a march, in the words of one agency lawyer, "scared the government half to death." President Roosevelt quickly issued an executive order banning race discrimination in defense industries and in the federal government.

The growing political power of northern blacks induced the president to appoint Benjamin O. Davis, Sr. as the first black general in American history, and William Hastie, already the nation's first black federal judge, as the civilian aide to the Secretary of War. The influence of black voters similarly inspired the House of Representatives to pass anti-poll-tax bills every two years in the 1940s, and in 1944, led Democratic Party bosses to veto the vice-presidential candidacy of Jimmy Byrnes, a former senator from South Carolina who held conventional southern views on white supremacy. Harry S. Truman, who ultimately received that nomination, had voted for antilynching and anti-poll-tax bills in the Senate.

World War II also created valuable economic opportunities for blacks. Military conscription produced labor shortages, which induced many war industries to relax their restrictions on hiring black workers. Unemployment among blacks fell from 937,000 in

1940 to 151,000 four years later, and the average income of urban black workers doubled. Black soldiers, though still suffering rampant discrimination, received skills training, education, and decent pay. War-related economic opportunities helped foster a black middle class, which proved instrumental to the postwar civil rights movement.

After the war, black soldiers returned home fighting for racial justice. Thousands of black veterans tried to register to vote, apparently sharing the view of one soldier that "[a]fter having been overseas fighting for democracy, I thought that when we got back here we should enjoy a little of it." Reflecting this new mood, a recently discharged black sailor in Columbia, Tennessee, beat up a white radio repairman who had cursed and struck his mother during a disagreement over a repair job. A race riot ensued.

Veterans were not the only blacks in a mood to fight for racial change. One white southerner observed with a sense of wonder, "It is as if some universal message had reached the great mass of Negroes, urging them to dream new dreams and to protest against the old order." An NAACP branch in Louisiana informed an obstructionist voter registrar that "you do not seem to realize that the social order [has] changed [now that] over ten thousand Negro men and women died in World War II for 'World Democracy.'"

Soon after World War II ended, the cold war began, and it too proved beneficial to the cause of progressive racial change. As Americans and Soviets competed for the allegiance of a predominantly nonwhite Third World, southern white supremacy became democracy's greatest vulnerability.

One State Department expert estimated that nearly half of all Soviet propaganda directed against the United States involved racial issues. In 1946 Soviet Foreign Minister V. M. Molotov asked Secretary of State Jimmy Byrnes how Americans could justify pressing the Soviets to conduct free elections in Poland when

America did not guarantee them in South Carolina or Georgia. In embracing civil rights, President Truman stressed "how closely our democracy is under observation," and he noted that "[t]he top dog in a world which is half colored ought to clean his own house."

The worldwide decolonization that followed the war also helped to inspire American blacks, who saw domestic racial reform as "part and parcel of the struggle against imperialism and exploitation in [the Third World]." Blacks hoped that if the principle of self-determination for colonized peoples could be established, an irresistible tide of change would sweep across the United States. In 1945 civil rights leaders attended the inaugural session of the United Nations with a dual agenda: racial equality at home and colonial self-determination abroad.

Actions taken by the federal government in the 1940s reveal dramatic changes in race relations. The Justice Department began prosecuting lynchings and submitting briefs in civil rights cases that urged the Supreme Court to strike down racial segregation and discrimination. President Truman appointed a civil rights committee, and then followed its recommendations by proposing landmark civil rights legislation and issuing executive orders desegregating the military and the federal civil service.

Important changes were also occurring outside of government. Baseball—the national pastime—was desegregated in 1946–47. By 1950 blacks were also playing in the National Football League and the National Basketball Association. The American Medical Association and the American Nurses Association accepted their first black members after the war. By the late 1940s, church leaders of most denominations were condemning racial segregation, and Hollywood films were beginning to confront racial issues, such as interracial marriage and lynching.

Racial reform was also occurring in the South, where black voter registration increased fourfold in the 1940s. Protection against police brutality was a top priority for blacks, and many southern cities hired their first black police officers since Reconstruction. Southern cities also began providing black communities with better public services and recreational facilities, and states increased their spending on black education.

Cracks in the walls of segregation began to appear in the peripheral South. In the late 1940s, Catholic parochial schools and public swimming pools desegregated in cities such as Baltimore, St. Louis, and Washington, D.C. Medical societies in these cities admitted their first blacks, and some theaters and lunch counters desegregated. In 1951 Maryland repealed its Jim Crow transportation law.

Other changes in racial practices penetrated even further into the South. College football games against integrated northern teams became more common throughout the South, and some formerly white southern universities allowed blacks onto their football teams. Minor league baseball teams were desegregated, even in the Deep South. In 1953 Ralph Bunche, the black American who won the Nobel Peace Prize for his work at the United Nations, spoke in unsegregated public auditoriums in Raleigh, Miami, and Atlanta. In New Orleans in the early 1950s, Catholic universities, public parks, and the public library were desegregated, and the first black Catholic priest in the Deep South was ordained.

Racial change was taking place in the North as well. In the late 1940s, hundreds of organizations devoted to civil rights reform were established in northern cities. Northern religious organizations condemned race discrimination, and foundations financed studies by social scientists into the causes and cures of racial prejudice. Legal research in support of civil rights litigation became a favorite pro bono project of students at the Columbia University School of Law.

Northern states and cities enacted a barrage of civil rights legislation after the war, including fair employment and public accommodations laws. A couple of northern states threatened to terminate financial support for school districts in violation of segregation prohibitions. These laws quickly forced the desegregation of schools in the southern counties of Illinois, Indiana, and New Jersey—several years before the Supreme Court confronted southern school segregation in *Brown v. Board of Education*.

Changing racial mores profoundly influenced the Court's racial jurisprudence. In *Smith v. Allwright* (1944), the justices voted eight to one to invalidate the white primary—a stunning reversal of a unanimous decision only nine years earlier. With African Americans dying on battlefields around the world, the justices must have been tempted to help move the nation, in the words of the *New York Times*, "a little nearer to a more perfect democracy, in which there will be but one class of citizens." Many southern whites now conceded that excluding blacks from the only elections that mattered in the South was a "cruel and shameful thing," which "profane[d] the Bill of Rights."

Smith helped to produce dramatic increases in black voter registration in the South. In Georgia the number of black registered voters rose from roughly 20,000 in 1940 to 125,000 in 1947; in Louisiana, the number increased from 8,000 in 1948 to 107,000 by 1952. Even in retrograde Mississippi, black voter registration increased from 2,500 in 1946 to 20,000 in 1950.

As black veterans took advantage of the GI Bill of Rights to apply to white universities, the justices confronted more cases involving segregation in higher education. When Heman Sweatt demanded admission to the all-white University of Texas School of Law in 1946, the state set up a separate black institution. In 1950 the Court ruled it inadequate and ordered Sweatt admitted to the white law school. In addition to noting the tangible features of the black school that were obviously inferior, such as the number of books in the library, the justices emphasized the inequality of intangible features of the two schools, such as the stature and influence of the alumni. Most contemporary observers, reasoning

Heman Sweatt (1912–1982), standing in line to register for classes at the University of Texas Law School in 1950

that such intangibles could never be equalized, concluded that *Sweatt* had nullified segregation in higher education.

On the same day as the ruling in *Sweatt*, the Court ordered the graduate education school of the University of Oklahoma to cease segregating—in classrooms, the library, and the cafeteria— George McLaurin, the black man it had admitted pursuant to federal court order. The justices declared that segregation restrictions impaired McLaurin's ability to learn his profession. As he was receiving an equal education in terms of tangible services, the decision suggests that the justices were no longer prepared to accept segregation *within* an institution of higher education. As *Sweatt* had proscribed segregation in *separate* institutions, that seemed to leave segregation nowhere to remain.

Despite the unanimous outcomes, several justices were troubled by the rulings in *Sweatt* and *McLaurin*. At conference, Chief Justice Fred M. Vinson denied that the original understanding of the Fourteenth Amendment covered public education, and he noted that numerous precedents had sustained separate-but-equal education. Stanley Reed likewise thought that it was "hard ... to say something that has been constitutional for years is suddenly bad. The 14th Amendment was not aimed at segregation." Justice Robert Jackson could "find no basis for [the] idea that [the] Fourteenth [Amendment] reached schools," and he worried that *Sweatt* required the Court not merely to "fill gaps or construe the amendment to include matters which were unconsidered" but "to include what was deliberately and intentionally excluded."

In tension with precedent and original understanding, these decisions are best explained in terms of social and political change. By 1950 major league baseball had been desegregated for several years, and the military was undergoing gradual desegregation. The Truman administration intervened in these cases, warning that "unless segregation is ended, a serious blow will be struck at our democracy before the world." The Court's first black law clerk, William T. Coleman, authored a memo to Justice Felix Frankfurter two years earlier urging that *Plessy* be overturned. Coleman's very presence at the Court demonstrated that segregated legal education could no longer be defended on the basis of supposed black inferiority.

Several justices apparently shared Jackson's conviction that "the segregation system [in higher education] is breaking down of its own weight and that a little time will end it in nearly all states." Two thousand white students and faculty members rallied in support of Sweatt's lawsuit against the University of Texas Law School. Opinion polls showed substantial—even majority—support among the university's students for integration, and faculty members overwhelmingly endorsed it. Thus, the justices could dismiss as groundless the warnings of white southerners that violence and school closures would ensue if Sweatt won his case. Within six months of the Court's ruling, roughly a thousand blacks were attending formerly white colleges and universities in the South, without causing any serious racial disturbances.

The postwar Court also considered a challenge to residential segregation. The dearth of new housing construction during the Great Depression and World War II, combined with the massive increases in urban populations resulting from internal migration, led to severe housing shortages. The problem was especially acute for blacks because in most northern cities a large percentage of housing stock was covered by racially restrictive covenants. Racial conflict over housing was pervasive and helped cause a deadly race riot in Detroit in 1943. By the end of World War II, hundreds of lawsuits throughout the nation sought to enforce racially restrictive covenants, while defendants challenged the constitutionality of judicial enforcement.

Precedent on this issue was unambiguous. Supreme Court dicta had denied that judicial enforcement of racially restrictive covenants was unconstitutional, and nineteen state supreme courts had reached the same conclusion. The clarity of precedent made Thurgood Marshall reluctant to press the issue in the high court, but he was unable to control the litigation.

Precedent notwithstanding, the Court in *Shelley v. Kraemer* (1948) barred the judicial enforcement of racially restrictive covenants. The Great Depression and the New Deal had drastically altered conceptions of government responsibility for conduct occurring in the "private" sphere. The Four Freedoms articulated in President Roosevelt's 1941 inaugural address included freedom "from want" and "from fear"—not typical negative liberties protected from government interference, but affirmative rights to government protection from privately inflicted harms. In 1947 President Truman invoked this notion of expanded government responsibility, declaring that "the extension of civil rights today means not protection of the people against the government, but protection of the people by the government." In *Shelley*, the justices responded to such changed understandings by imposing constitutional constraints on race discrimination that occurred in what had traditionally been regarded as the private sphere.

Perhaps even more important to the outcome in *Shelley* were changes in racial attitudes. As one newspaper observed, "[A] nation that has poured out its blood and treasure in a war billed as a contest against racism can hardly afford the luxury of forcing its own citizens to live in ghettos." *Shelley* was decided the same year that a national civil rights consciousness crystallized. Earlier in 1948 President Truman had introduced landmark civil rights proposals, and the issue of civil rights played a significant role in the presidential election that fall. Moreover, restrictive covenants, unlike many racial issues, directly impacted other minority groups—

Jews, Asians, Latinos, Native Americans—whose collective interests were likely to command the attention of New Deal justices.

Shelley opened up significant new housing opportunities for blacks, but it had almost no impact on residential segregation. Urban whites often moved to suburbs as blacks entered their neighborhoods, and blacks were generally not free to follow them there. Banks denied loans to blacks seeking to purchase homes in white areas. Incredibly, for two years after *Shelley*, the Federal Housing Administration continued to encourage the use of racially restrictive covenants and to discourage black movement into white neighborhoods.

Local governments building public housing after the war ensured that it was racially segregated, and courts did not intervene against that practice until the late 1960s. Private real estate developers who were building enormous suburban housing complexes tended to exclude blacks entirely. Levittown, Pennsylvania, was home to sixty thousand whites—and not a single black—when it opened in the 1950s. Most real estate agents refused to show blacks homes in white neighborhoods—a practice that their code of professional responsibility mandated until 1950.

The few blacks who surmounted such barriers and bought homes in white neighborhoods often faced mob violence. Blacks moving into white neighborhoods in Miami after the war endured cross burnings, Klan bombings, police harassment, and arson. So many homes bought by black families in contested neighborhoods in Birmingham, Alabama, were bombed that one such area became known as "Dynamite Hill." When a black family moved into a white apartment complex in the Chicago suburb of Cicero in 1951, a mob consisting of thousands of angry whites, including the police chief and the chairman of the town council, drove them out.

Even as many whites became generally supportive of civil rights after the war, they continued to favor residential segregation. This was as true of whites in the North as in the South. Because racially restrictive covenants were just one of many methods for maintaining housing segregation, *Shelley* had almost no integrative effect. The justices declined to delve deeper into the problem of residential segregation, refusing even to review a New York case involving the exclusion of blacks from a large private housing development that had been constructed with the assistance of tax breaks and use of the eminent domain power.

The one glaring exception to the Court's growing progressivism on race involved the treatment of persons of Japanese descent during World War II. The Japanese attack on Pearl Harbor in December 1941 led to a panic over a possible Japanese invasion of the United States. Politicians and military leaders began to demand the relocation and internment of Japanese living on the West Coast, two-thirds of whom were American citizens. The drumbeat of support for internment quickened as Japanese military forces swept through Southeast Asia and a special presidential commission blamed Japanese saboteurs in Hawaii for the debacle at Pearl Harbor.

In February 1942 President Roosevelt issued an executive order authorizing exclusion and internment. The military imposed a curfew on Japanese living on the West Coast. Soon thereafter, it ordered them to report to relocation centers, from where they were transported to internment camps, in which most of them—about 120,000 persons—spent the duration of the war. By voice vote, Congress made it a crime to resist an exclusion order. Reflecting public anxiety over the possible disloyalty of Japanese Americans, a deeply divided American Civil Liberties Union initially declined to challenge the legality of exclusion and internment.

The proffered justification for these extraordinary measures was national security: it was argued that some Japanese Americans were disloyal and thus likely to commit espionage and sabotage. Moreover, in the event of a Japanese invasion, it would be impossible to quickly distinguish the invaders from Japanese Americans.

Despite such justifications, racial prejudice played a critical role in the internment. The Japanese, like the Chinese before them, had long endured virulent discrimination on the West Coast. They were segregated in schools, barred from various occupations, denied the right to own real estate, subjected to vigilante violence, and made ineligible for American citizenship unless born in the United States.

After Pearl Harbor, organizations of Caucasian farmers, who resented competition from hard-working Japanese fruit and vegetable growers, seized the opportunity to be rid of their rivals. The representative of one such association candidly told Congress, "We're charged with wanting to get rid of the Japs for selfish reasons. We might as well be honest. We do. It's a question of whether the white man lives on the Pacific Coast or the brown man."

General John DeWitt, author of the exclusion order, told Congress that "a Jap is a Jap" and that the Japanese must be "wiped off the map." Governors of western states, such as Idaho and Wyoming, rejected proposals to relocate the Japanese to farms within their states, insisting that the Japanese remain behind barbed wire. One governor warned, "If you bring the Japanese into my state, I promise you they will be hanging from every tree."

Long after the military ceased to claim any national security justification for continued exclusion of the Japanese from the West Coast, President Roosevelt refused to authorize their return for fear that it would cost him California's electoral votes in the 1944 presidential contest. When the military exclusion order was revoked in December 1944, the *Los Angeles Times* called the decision a "grave mistake," and public officials on the West Coast warned that returning Japanese would face vigilante riots. Polls taken that year in Los Angeles revealed that 74 percent of respondents favored a constitutional amendment to deport all Japanese after the war.

The Supreme Court failed to curb the anti-Japanese hysteria. In 1943 the justices unanimously rejected a constitutional challenge to the Japanese curfew. In 1944 in *Korematsu v. United States*, a divided Court sustained the constitutionality of the exclusion order. The War Department failed to inform the justices that its own counterintelligence reports had concluded that the risks of Japanese espionage and sabotage were too trivial to justify wholesale internment. Given the tenor of the times, there is reason to doubt whether the disclosure of this information would have affected the outcome of the case.

Most Japanese Americans spent most of the war behind barbed wire. Conditions in the internment camps were harsh; tem-

Fred Korematsu (1919–2005)

peratures tended to be extremely hot in the summer and bitterly cold in the winter. Thousands of Japanese, disillusioned and embittered, applied for repatriation to Japan.

Thousands more left the camps to serve in the U.S. Army, many compiling magnificent service records. Those refusing to serve once conscripted were sent to prison. A federal judge who sentenced sixty-three Japanese American draft resisters to three years in prison apiece remarked, "If they are truly loyal American citizens they should embrace ... the opportunity to discharge the duties [of citizenship] by offering themselves in the cause of our National Defense."

Perhaps eager to redeem themselves, the justices after the war applied the era's budding racial progressivism to the Japanese. In two 1948 rulings, the Court effectively interred California's alien land law, which barred Japanese from owning real estate, and it invalidated a California statute prohibiting Japanese aliens from securing fishing licenses.

Reflecting the same combination of guilt and postwar racial enlightenment, Congress in 1948 provided compensation—albeit grossly inadequate—for property losses suffered by the Japanese as a result of exclusion and internment. In 1952 Congress ended the ban on Japanese immigration and made U.S. residents of Japanese descent eligible for citizenship—steps it had taken during the war for Chinese because China was a war ally.

The postwar wave of racial progressivism also influenced the behavior of lower court judges and state legislators. Court decisions in New Mexico and Arizona struck down voting restrictions that had previously disfranchised most Native Americans. In 1946 a federal judge invalidated the segregation of Mexican Americans in several southern California school districts. That same year the California legislature repealed the statute authorizing school segregation for Asians. In 1947 the Utah legislature repealed its alien land law. In 1948 the California Supreme Court invalidated the state's ban on interracial marriage.

In 1952 black leader Lester Granger detected "a social malleability in the South today that has not been equaled since during the days of Reconstruction." Fifteen years earlier, many blacks had doubted whether their grandchildren would live to see an end to segregation. Now, however, the question seemed to be whether segregation would meet its demise this year or next.

Earlier, black leaders had disagreed among themselves over aims, tactics, and strategies. Some preferred to work for integration; others sought genuine equality within a segregated system. Some believed that litigation was an effective method of achieving social change; others had grave doubts.

Such disagreements were largely made moot by the integrationist ideology of the war and by the impressive legal victories of the NAACP. Black leaders now converged behind an all-out legal assault on segregation that would have been inconceivable just a few years earlier.

For their part, white southerners were beginning to recognize the looming threat posed to segregation, and they warned of dire consequences should legal challenges prove successful. Indeed, suits challenging segregation in public grade schools were already under way in several southern and border states. How would the justices respond, and how would white southerners react should the Court vindicate those challenges?

CHAPTER NINE

Brown v. Board of Education

IN THE SPRING OF 1951, black students at segregated Moton High School in Prince Edward County, Virginia, commenced a strike against overcrowding and inadequate facilities in their school. Local leaders of the NAACP initially tried to discourage the protest because rural southern Virginia seemed like such an inhospitable environment in which to challenge Jim Crow education. When the students would not be dissuaded, however, the association's lawyers agreed to sponsor a lawsuit, but only on the condition that the students directly challenge segregation. This lawsuit was consolidated with four other cases into what has become known to history as *Brown v. Board of Education.*

The justices of the Supreme Court were unenthusiastic about confronting so soon the issue they had deliberately evaded in 1950. Moreover, these lawsuits were unrepresentative of the school segregation issue. Three were from jurisdictions—Kansas, Delaware, and the District of Columbia—where whites were not intransigently committed to segregation, and judicial invalidation would probably not cause great disruption. The other two cases, however, came from Clarendon County, South Carolina, and Prince Edward County, Virginia, where blacks were 70 percent and 45 percent of the populations, respectively. Broad forces for racial change had barely touched these counties, where a judicial ban on school segregation might well jeopardize public education.

Yet, ironically, the NAACP's decision in 1950 to no longer accept school equalization cases had pushed blacks in these counties to convert their grievances against inferior schools into broad challenges to segregation. The association was unwilling to abandon courageous blacks who challenged Jim Crow under oppressive conditions, but it did pressure them to attack segregation directly. Some civil rights advocates questioned the wisdom of pressing a desegregation suit on the Court at this time. Why run the risk, they wondered, if narrower challenges to racial inequality were virtually certain to succeed?

On May 17, 1954, the Court unanimously invalidated racial segregation in public grade schools. The decision emphasized the importance of public education in modern life and refused to be bound by the original understanding of the Fourteenth Amendment, which had not condemned segregation.

That the ruling was unanimous does not mean that *Brown* was easy. In a memorandum written the day *Brown* was decided, Justice William O. Douglas observed that a vote taken after the case was first argued would have been "five to four in favor of the constitutionality of segregation in the public schools." Justice Felix Frankfurter reported that such a vote would have been five to four to *invalidate* segregation.

Brown was hard for many of the justices because their legal views and their personal views conflicted. The sources of constitutional interpretation to which they ordinarily looked for guidance—the text of the Constitution, its original understanding, judicial precedent, and custom—seemed to validate school segregation. By contrast, most of the justices personally condemned segregation, which Justice Hugo Black called "Hitler's creed."

Justice Frankfurter regularly preached that judges must decide cases on "the compulsions of governing legal principles," not "the idiosyncrasies of a merely personal judgment." That he abhorred racial segregation is clear. In the 1930s Frankfurter had served on the NAACP's legal committee, and in 1948 he had hired the Court's first black law clerk, William Coleman.

Yet Frankfurter had trouble finding a compelling legal argument to invalidate segregation. His law clerk, Alexander Bickel, read the entire legislative history of the Fourteenth Amendment and reported that it was "impossible" to conclude that its supporters had intended to abolish school segregation. To be sure, Frankfurter believed that the meaning of constitutional concepts can change with evolving social mores, but in 1954, public schools in twenty-one states and the District of Columbia were still segregated.

Furthermore, judicial precedent, which Frankfurter called "the most influential factor in giving a society coherence and continuity," strongly supported school segregation. Of forty-four challenges to that practice adjudicated by lower courts between 1865 and 1935, not one had succeeded. On the basis of legislative history and precedent, Frankfurter conceded that "*Plessy* is right."

Brown presented a similar dilemma for Justice Robert H. Jackson. In 1950 Jackson, who had left the Court for a year to prosecute Nazis at Nuremberg, wrote to a friend: "You and I have seen the terrible consequences of racial hatred in Germany. We can have no sympathy with racial conceits which underlie segregation policies." Yet, like Frankfurter, Jackson thought that judges were obliged to separate their personal views from the law.

Justice Robert H. Jackson (1892–1954)

Jackson revealed his internal struggles in a draft opinion that began: "Decision of these cases would be simple if our personal opinion that school segregation is morally, economically or politically indefensible made it legally so." But when Jackson turned to the question of whether existing law condemned segregation, he had difficulty answering in the affirmative:

> Layman as well as lawyer must query how it is that the Constitution this morning forbids what for three-quarters of a century it has tolerated or approved.... Convenient as it would be to reach an opposite conclusion, I simply cannot find in the conventional material of constitutional interpretation any justification for saying that ... segregated schools ... violate[] the Fourteenth Amendment.

That some of these nine justices were uneasy about invalidating segregation is unsurprising. They were put on the Court to repudiate, in Jackson's words, "the old court['s] ... unjustified judicial control over social and economic affairs." Thus, several of them shared Chief Justice Fred Vinson's view that "it would be better if [Congress] would act." Jackson cautioned, "However desirable it may be to abolish educational segregation, we cannot ... ignore the question whether the use of judicial office to initiate law reforms that cannot get enough national public support to put them through Congress, is our own constitutional function."

Fearing irreconcilable differences, the justices decided to postpone resolution of the cases until the following year. Then, in September 1953, Chief Justice Vinson died suddenly of a heart attack. President Dwight D. Eisenhower appointed Governor Earl Warren of California to replace him.

At the conference following the reargument of *Brown*, Warren opened the discussion by announcing that he could not "see how segregation can be justified in this day and age." Anyone counting heads would have immediately recognized that the outcome was no longer in doubt. Warren, together with the four justices who had declared school segregation unconstitutional the preceding year, made a majority for that outcome.

With the result settled, two factors encouraged unanimity. First, the justices understood that white southerners would exploit any hint of internal Court dissension to further their resistance to school desegregation. Justices who disagreed with the outcome in *Brown* thus felt pressure to suppress their convictions for the good of the institution.

Second, after Warren had provided a fifth vote to condemn segregation, ambivalent justices such as Frankfurter and Jackson were irrelevant to the outcome, whereas a year earlier they had controlled it. They might have allowed their legal interpretations to trump their personal predilections if it affected the outcome, but not for the sake of a dissent.

How were the most conflicted justices able to overcome their doubts and vote to invalidate segregation? All judicial decision making involves both legal and extralegal—or "political"—considerations; the latter include influences such as the judges' personal values, social mores, and external political pressure. When the law is clear, judges will generally follow it. And in 1954, the law—as understood by most of the justices—was reasonably clear. Neither the text of the Fourteenth Amendment nor its original understanding condemned segregation; precedent and custom strongly supported it. For the justices to reject a result so clearly indicated by the conventional legal sources suggests that they had very strong personal views to the contrary.

And so they did. As the justices deliberated over *Brown*, they expressed astonishment at—and approval of—the extent of the recent changes in racial mores. Minton detected "a different world today" with regard to race. Frankfurter remarked that "the pace of progress has surprised even those most eager in its promotion." Jackson, declaring that "Negro progress ... has been spectacular," concluded that segregation "has outlived whatever justification it may have had."

Justice Frankfurter later conceded that had the issue arisen in the 1940s, he would have voted to uphold school segregation because "public opinion had not then crystallized against it." The justices in *Brown* understood that they were reinforcing and enhancing—not creating—a movement for racial reform.

Brown declared public school segregation unconstitutional, but it imposed no immediate remedy, deferring that issue to the following year. In *Brown II*, decided on May 31, 1955, the justices remanded the cases to district courts with instructions to require a "prompt and reasonable start toward full compliance," with additional time allowed if "consistent with good faith compliance at the earliest practicable date." The parties to the litigation were to be admitted to public schools on a nondiscriminatory basis "with all deliberate speed," rather than immediately, as the NAACP had sought.

Several factors may account for this temporizing result. An informal deal had enabled the Court to be unanimous in *Brown I;* several justices had insisted on gradualism as their price for voting to invalidate segregation, and now the quid pro quo had to be paid. The justices also feared issuing unenforceable orders, which could injure the Court by revealing its weakness, and they worried that immediate desegregation would cause violence and school closures. Some of the justices may have favored gradualism because they felt guilty about undermining the expectations of white southerners who had assumed the legitimacy of separate-but-equal based on prior Court rulings. Finally, several justices believed that they could defuse resistance among southern whites by appearing accommodating.

Many white southerners interpreted *Brown II* as a sign of the justices' weakness. A Florida segregationist thought the Court had "realized it made a mistake . . . and is getting out of it the best way it can." A Texas legislator declared that the "Court got hold of a hot potato and didn't know what to do with it." Many southern whites believed that their threats of school closures and violence had intimidated the justices, and they now predicted that determined resistance would convince the Court and the nation to abandon southern blacks, as they had during Reconstruction.

Did the justices' miscalculation in *Brown II* matter much? Probably not. Even an order for immediate desegregation would have been bitterly resisted. Most white southerners would oppose desegregation until they were convinced that resistance was costly and futile. The Court was powerless to make that showing on its own.

The justices backed off after *Brown II*, waiting for some signal of support from Congress or the president. They waited a long time. President Eisenhower repeatedly refused to say whether he thought *Brown* was rightly decided. He preached moderation, urged that desegregation difficulties be resolved locally, and repeated the mantra of southern whites that "it is difficult through law and through force to change a man's heart."

Congress did not support the Court either. Throughout the 1950s, liberal congressional representatives failed even in their efforts to pass symbolic statements affirming that *Brown* was the law of the land. Congress did finally pass weak civil rights legislation in 1957 but without a proposed provision to empower the attorney general to bring desegregation suits. The tepid commitment of politicians to the enforcement of *Brown* was mirrored by that of their constituents: polls revealed that national majorities of nearly four to one preferred gradualism to immediate action.

The Court briefly reentered the fray during the Little Rock crisis. In September 1957, after Governor Orval Faubus of Arkansas used the state militia to block enforcement of a court desegregation order, President Eisenhower sent in the army's 101st Airborne Division to implement the decree. Several blacks attended Central High School under military guard during the 1957–58 school year.

The situation was chaotic. Hundreds of white students were suspended for harassing blacks, and there were more than twenty bomb threats. Early in 1958 the Little Rock school board petitioned the federal district judge for a reprieve of two and a half years to allow community resistance to subside. He granted it.

The court of appeals reversed, and the justices convened in special summer session to determine whether a district judge could delay school desegregation, once it had begun, because of community resistance.

Cooper v. Aaron (1958) was not difficult for the justices, who understood that rewarding violent resistance in Little Rock by postponing desegregation would encourage similar behavior elsewhere. In a forceful opinion, the Court dressed down Faubus and the Arkansas legislature.

But the apparent boldness of the interventions by the president and the Court was misleading. Eisenhower had used federal troops only after a governor's blatant defiance of a desegregation order. The justices had acted primarily to support the president. Neither party had abandoned gradualism.

In 1958–59, the Court took two noteworthy actions on school desegregation. First, the justices summarily affirmed a lower court decision that rejected a challenge to Alabama's pupil placement law, which evaded desegregation by authorizing administrators to place students in schools according to a long list of ostensibly race-neutral factors. Second, the justices denied review of a lower court decision rejecting a challenge to Nashville's desegregation plan, which authorized racial mixing in one additional grade per year and allowed students to transfer from assigned schools if their racial group was in the minority.

White southerners were jubilant. Governor John Patterson of Alabama saw "an indication that the Supreme Court is going to let us handle our own affairs," and Senator Russell Long of Louisiana detected "a willingness of the court to settle for token integration." One prominent southern journalist wrote that the Court "begins to see that massive integration won't work," and he urged southern whites to embrace token desegregation to enable the justices to "save face."

The justices' thinking can be reconstructed with some guesswork. Between 1957 and 1959, southern battle lines were drawn around outright defiance of *Brown* and token compliance; the extremism of post-*Brown* southern politics had eliminated meaningful integration as an option.

Eisenhower's use of troops at Little Rock demonstrated to the South that schools could not remain segregated after courts had ordered them desegregated. But did they have to remain open? Massive resisters had been threatening to close schools as their final resort since 1954. After Little Rock, they were put to the test. In 1958 Governor Faubus of Arkansas and Governor Lindsay Almond of Virginia closed several schools that courts had ordered desegregated. Other southern states watched attentively to see how events would unfold.

Meanwhile, "moderate" southern politicians fought to keep schools open by promising to restrict integration to token levels. In 1957 Republican Ted Dalton ran for governor of Virginia, repudiating school closures and endorsing the use of pupil placement schemes to limit integration. That same year Governor Leroy Collins of Florida insisted that some desegregation was inevitable but promised that it could be delayed and controlled through the pupil placement law. In 1958 Malcolm Seawell, the attorney general of North Carolina, endorsed similar policies.

These were risky positions for southern politicians to take. Dalton was labeled "an integrationist." Collins was attacked for "surrendering" and called a "weakling." Seawell was pilloried for his "abject surrender" and compared to Judas Iscariot.

For the Court to have invalidated token desegregation measures at this time might have destroyed these moderate politicians. Diehard segregationists would have seized upon such rulings as proof that no middle ground existed between massive resistance and massive integration. Since 1954 the justices had sought to bolster southern moderates, many of whom were explicitly appealing to the Court after Little Rock for a "cooling off" period. The justices' actions in 1958–59 suggest that they were not deaf to such appeals.

The executive branch did nothing to discourage the justices from reaffirming gradualism. In August 1958 President Eisenhower denied a magazine report that he had privately criticized *Brown*, while admitting that he might have "said something about 'slower.'" (Thurgood Marshall quipped in response, "If we slow down any more, we'll be going backward.") Editing a desegregation speech of his attorney general, William Rogers, Eisenhower urged Rogers to refrain from suggesting that integration "will necessarily be permanent" and to hint that an acceptable desegregation plan need not be completed within ten years. In 1960, with fewer than one black child in a thousand attending school with whites in the South, Rogers made the extraordinary statement that the pace of desegregation is "surprisingly good when compared with the legal problems involved."

Although large cities in border South states, such as Baltimore and St. Louis, desegregated schools almost immediately after *Brown*, the eleven states of the former Confederacy responded very differently. As late as 1960, only 98 of Arkansas's 104,000 black students attended school with whites, 34 of North Carolina's 302,000, and 103 of Virginia's 203,000. In the five states of the Deep South, not one of the 1.4 million black schoolchildren attended a racially mixed school until the fall of 1960. Three years later, just 1.06 percent of southern black children attended school with whites. How could *Brown* have been so ineffective for so long?

Because the Court's ruling technically bound school boards in only the five consolidated cases, litigation was necessary in every southern school district—of which there were thousands—in which education officials declined to voluntarily desegregate. Most school board members undoubtedly thought that *Brown* was wrongheaded, as did most white southerners, so their inclinations were to delay and evade as much as possible. School board members had additional incentives to avoid compliance with *Brown:* those responsible for desegregating schools received hate mail, had crosses burned on their lawns, suffered economic reprisals, and even endured physical violence.

School board members faced little pressure from the opposite direction. Until local litigation produced a desegregation order, they ran no risk of being held in contempt of court. Criminal prosecution and civil damages actions were also unlikely, as defendants in such suits have a right to a jury trial, and white jurors were unlikely to convict public officials for resisting desegregation.

Given these circumstances, few school boards chose desegregation until courts ordered them to do so. Thus, the implementation of *Brown* depended on the ability of black parents to bring lawsuits and on the willingness of federal judges to order desegregation. Neither condition was easily satisfied.

Because few blacks could afford to litigate, virtually all desegregation litigation involved the NAACP. Comprehending this, southern whites declared war on the association. States passed laws requiring disclosure of NAACP membership lists, which would expose members to economic and physical reprisals. Private segregationist organizations ensured that known NAACP members lost their jobs, credit, and suppliers. More than one lawyer representing the association in school desegregation litigation had his home bombed.

Even when the NAACP financed litigation, it still had to locate plaintiffs. In the Deep South, few blacks volunteered. Many blacks who had signed school desegregation petitions in 1954–55 suffered swift and severe retribution, which deterred prospective litigants. Not a single black in Mississippi sued for grade school desegregation until 1963. (One of the plaintiffs in that lawsuit, Medgar Evers, was quickly assassinated.) In Georgia and Alabama, the first desegregation suits outside of the largest cities were not filed until 1962–63. Ironically, suits proliferated in border states where desegregation was already farthest along.

Litigation could only bring the issue before a judge, who would have to determine whether, when, and how schools would desegregate. In 1954 all southern federal judges were white, and their views on school desegregation were mostly similar to those of other white southerners. Many were openly disdainful of *Brown*, and almost none publicly endorsed it. Judge George Bell Timmerman of South Carolina stated a typical view: whites "still have the right to choose their own companions and associates, and to preserve the integrity of the race with which God Almighty has endowed them."

Even those judges who were less viscerally hostile to *Brown* could be influenced by the disapprobation of friends and colleagues and by the violence of vigilantes. One federal judge ordering desegregation saw the grave of his son desecrated, and another endured the bombing of his mother's home.

Even when judges eventually ordered desegregation, most of them endorsed gradualism and tokenism. Pupil placement laws gave administrators discretion to allocate students according to a list of racially neutral factors. Refusing to presume that such discretion was exercised in a discriminatory way, lower courts generally declined to invalidate such laws on their face, and the Supreme Court concurred. Districts opting for neighborhood schools generally offered liberal transfer options that drastically curtailed desegregation, and most courts sustained these plans well into the 1960s.

When Congress passed the 1964 Civil Rights Act, fewer than two black children in a hundred attended a racially mixed school in the South. The federal judiciary, acting without significant support from either Congress or the president, had failed to accomplish more.

Brown mattered in ways other than directly placing black children in racially mixed schools. Major newspapers heralded the ruling in front-page, banner headlines. A 1955 poll found that 60 percent of white southerners had discussed *Brown* within the preceding week. *Brown* forced people to think about—and take a position on—school segregation.

Brown also had enormous symbolic significance for African Americans. One black newspaper stated a widely shared view—*Brown* was "the greatest victory for the Negro people since the Emancipation Proclamation." One black leader called *Brown* "a majestic break in the dark clouds," and another later recalled that blacks "literally got out and danced in the streets."

Brown motivated blacks to challenge the racial status quo. At the NAACP's urging, southern blacks in hundreds of localities petitioned school boards for immediate desegregation on threat of litigation. In the mid-1950s, but for *Brown*, such challenges would have been inconceivable in the Deep South, where one might have predicted that a campaign for racial reform would begin with demands for voting rights or the equalization of black schools.

Although *Brown* encouraged litigation, it may have discouraged direct-action racial protest. The NAACP's enormous Court victory encouraged blacks to litigate, not to protest in the streets. *Brown* also elevated the stature of the NAACP among blacks, and for the last fifty years, the association had favored litigation and lobbying, not direct-action protest. The NAACP had a vested interest in discouraging alternative strategies of protest that it could not monopolize, and it was composed of lawyers, who by nature were disinclined to march in the streets. In the late 1950s, the NAACP leadership rejected repeated requests from branches that the association supplement its traditional strategies with direct action protest.

The NAACP's predominant focus on litigation was myopic. Litigation encouraged blacks to sit back and allow elite lawyers and white judges to transform race relations rather than convincing them that they could make meaningful contributions to racial change themselves. Litigation was also limited in its capacity to generate the sort of conflict and violence that ultimately proved indispensable to transforming national opinion on race.

Although *Brown* may have briefly delayed direct action by encouraging litigation, this consequence of the decision was self-correcting: it quickly became clear that litigation without a social movement to support it could not produce significant social change. Thus, *Brown* may have eventually inspired direct action by raising the hopes and expectations of blacks, which litigation then proved incapable of fulfilling. Alternative forms of protest arose to fill the gap.

Many contemporaries identified precisely this link between black frustration over the pace of court-ordered desegregation and the explosion of direct-action protest in 1960. That year, the NAACP's annual convention declared the youth protests "symptomatic of the growing impatience of Negro Americans with the injustices of segregation and snail-like pace of desegregation." One black leader defended direct action on the ground that "we've had test cases and we've won them all and the status remains quo."

Brown contributed to direct-action protest in another way as well. After 1954 southern whites tried—with considerable success—to put the NAACP out of business. Alabama shut down NAACP operations in the state for eight years, and Louisiana and Texas did so for briefer periods. Nearly 250 southern branches closed.

With the NAACP under assault, southern blacks had no choice but to support alternative protest organizations. Black ministers, many of whom held prominent positions in NAACP branches, formed new groups, such as the Southern Christian Leadership Conference (SCLC). Such organizations used the NAACP's base of supporters, but they deployed their resources differently. Thus, by inciting massive retaliation against the NAACP, *Brown* ironically fostered new organizations that lacked the association's institutional and philosophical biases against direct action.

Brown had another, possibly more important consequence: virtually every year after 1954, school desegregation generated violent resistance somewhere in the South. These episodes tarnished the national image of white southerners, revealing "quiet, resolute Negro children defying jeers and violence and sadism."

In February 1956 a mob numbering over a thousand, throwing rocks and eggs and threatening a lynching, drove a black woman, Autherine Lucy, out of the University of Alabama. A South Carolina newspaper called the riot "a public disgrace," which has "played right into the hands of professional South-baiters." Compared with the mob, blacks had been models "of discipline, patience, and understanding." The *Washington Post* predicted that the incident would "outrage opinion even in areas where extreme views against integration prevail." Roy Wilkins, executive secretary of the NAACP, called for civil rights legislation to protect against mob violence and to withhold federal funds from educational institutions that defied *Brown*.

The desegregation riot in Little Rock, Arkansas, in September 1957 was a much larger affair, lasting for weeks and culminating in the use of federal troops. Outside of the South, public opinion overwhelmingly condemned the mob violence. Governor Faubus was widely ridiculed—"the sputtering sputnik from the Ozarks," according to Maryland Governor Theodore McKeldin. The NAACP's Gloster Current "thank[ed] God for Governor Faubus. He has hastened integration five years by opening the eyes of the country to the kind of thinking that will call out the National Guard to keep nine Negro students out of Little Rock High School." Wilkins similarly labeled Faubus "a valuable enemy" who has "aroused and educated to our point of view millions of people in America."

In November 1960 similarly ugly scenes unfolded in New Orleans. Night after night, nationwide television audiences watched hundreds of vicious protestors, their faces contorted by hate, spitting, snarling, and yelling obscenities—such as "kill them niggers"—at black six-year-olds walking to school in their Sunday best. The author John Steinbeck, who happened to be traveling through New Orleans at the time, called the mob's rantings "bestial and filthy and degenerate." The *New York Times*, which thought that the effort of "a racist rabble ... to subvert the Constitution and substitute anarchy for law" was "degrading and dangerous," warned that "[t]he conscience of America" would not tolerate the "mobsters." A Miami woman reported that "the appalling sight and sound ... [made her] sick—almost physically ill," while a German-born doctor compared the scenes to those enacted in Nazi Germany.

Much of the white-on-black violence in the South after 1954 occurred in the context of court-ordered school desegregation. To the extent that such violence helped transform national opinion on race, *Brown* was directly responsible.

Brown also crystallized southern whites' resistance to racial change, radicalized southern politics, and increased the likelihood that direct-action protest, once it erupted, would incite a violent response. Opinion polls conducted after *Brown* revealed that 15 to 25 percent of southern whites admitted to supporting violence, if necessary, to resist desegregation. One Ku Klux Klan leader reported that *Brown* created "a situation loaded with dynamite" and "really gave us a push." Now that the justices had "abolished the

Mason Dixon line," Klansmen vowed "to establish the Smith and Wesson line." In 1957 six Birmingham Klansmen castrated a randomly selected black man after taunting him for "think[ing] nigger kids should go to school with [white] kids."

Most southern politicians avoided explicit exhortations to violence, but the incendiary rhetoric they used to condemn *Brown* probably encouraged it. Congressman James Davis of Georgia insisted that "[t]here is no place for violence or lawless acts," but only after he had called *Brown* "a monumental fraud which is shocking, outrageous and reprehensible" and denied any obligation on "the people to bow the neck to this new form of tyranny." Senator James Eastland of Mississippi incited listeners with reminders that "[t]here is no law that a free people must submit to a flagrant invasion of their personal liberty" before cautioning that "[a]cts of violence and lawlessless have no place."

Brown desegregated few schools before 1964, but it nonetheless played a critical role in America's racial transformation. The decision raised the hopes and expectations of African Americans, which were then largely dashed by the South's massive resistance, thus revealing the limited capacity of litigation alone to produce meaningful social change. *Brown* inspired southern whites to try to destroy the NAACP, which unintentionally forced blacks to support alternative protest organizations that embraced philosophies more sympathetic to direct action. *Brown* created concrete occasions for white-on-black violence that tarnished the national image of southern whites. Finally, the southern political backlash ignited by *Brown* ensured that once civil rights demonstrators appeared on the streets, they were brutally suppressed. It was the televised beatings of peaceful black demonstrators by southern white law enforcement officers that repulsed national opinion and led directly to the passage of landmark civil rights legislation.

CHAPTER TEN

The Civil Rights Era

IN APRIL 1959 Mack Charles Parker, a black man who was scheduled to stand trial for raping a white woman, was seized from jail by a white mob in Poplarville, Mississippi, and lynched. One Mississippi newspaper blamed the Supreme Court's ruling in *Brown*, concluding that "force must not be used in pushing revolutionary changes in social custom. Every such action produces equal and opposite reaction." The judge presiding over the grand jury that investigated the lynching urged the jurors to "have the backbone to stand against any tyranny ... [even including] the Board of Sociology setting [*sic*] in Washington, garbed in Judicial Robes, and 'dishing out' the 'legal precedents' of Gunnar Myrdal [the Swedish social scientist whose work critical of race discrimination had been cited in *Brown*]."

White southerners worried that Parker's lynching would harm the cause of white supremacy. Governor James Coleman of Mississippi condemned the murder and hoped that Mississippians "won't be punished by civil rights legislation for what a handful

Mack Parker (1936–1959)

have done." Judge Tom Brady, a leading Mississippi segregationist, predicted that the NAACP would "rejoice in this highly regrettable incident" and "urge passage of vicious civil rights measures."

Brady was at least partially right. Roy Wilkins of the NAACP called Parker's lynching "the natural consequence of an organized campaign of law defiance" by southern politicians that demonstrated "the necessity of further and stronger protection of civil rights ... by the federal government." Attorney General William P. Rogers announced that he was studying the need for new civil rights legislation in light of Parker's lynching and the unwillingness of a grand jury to indict known participants, which he thought a flagrant injustice.

As the political backlash fomented by *Brown* generated more violent resistance to progressive racial change, northerners watched in horror and grew more determined to end southern white supremacy.

On December 5, 1955, blacks in Montgomery, Alabama, protesting the humiliating treatment they endured on city buses, decided to stop riding them. The boycott lasted an entire year and became a pivotal event in the history of American race relations.

The Montgomery bus boycott demonstrated to the world that ordinary black southerners were fed up with the racial status quo and were prepared to fight it, even at the cost of extreme personal hardship. The boycott also helped to convince individual blacks that through collective action they could transform social conditions. In the words of its organizers, the Montgomery movement marked "the passage of southern Negroes from an attitude of servility and passivity to a spirit of solidarity, fearlessness and hope."

The skill, fortitude, and courage with which blacks organized and executed the boycott contravened southern white stereotypes of black ineptitude, laziness, and timidity. Montgomery whites had never seen blacks "organize and discipline themselves, to carry something out to a finish," and they were consequently "very much impressed by their determination and courage." Blacks, not immune from being influenced by white stereotypes, were impressed as well.

The boycott also demonstrated the tactical value of nonviolent protest. The quiet dignity with which Montgomery blacks protested their racial oppression virtually ensured that white opponents, who used economic reprisals, trumped-up criminal charges, and even bombings, would face a damning indictment in the eyes of observers. Thousands of dollars in financial support (as well as many shoes) poured in from around the country, and supporters participated in a national "deliverance day of prayer" to demonstrate solidarity with Montgomery blacks.

A similar bus boycott had taken place in June 1953 in Baton Rouge, Louisiana, but it had ended after only one week, when the city council offered a compromise that was acceptable to black leaders. Yet Montgomery's public officials, rather than compromising, became increasingly intransigent. They adopted a "get tough" policy, arresting boycott organizers on fabricated charges and failing to suppress violence against boycott leaders.

In the wake of *Brown*, southern whites tended to view all racial issues against the backdrop of school desegregation. Thus, the Montgomery mayor, W. A. Gayle, declared that what blacks really wanted was "to destroy our whole social fabric," and another local segregationist called the bus demands "piddling stuff," as compared with the NAACP's real objectives: complete integration and interracial marriage. In such an environment, whites refused to make even minimal concessions to black demands. As a result, the boycott continued for a year, ultimately producing desegregation of the city's buses, which was more than the protestors originally sought.

After Montgomery, little direct-action protest against race discrimination took place in the South until 1960, when the region exploded with such activity. On February 1, four black college students sat in at the segregated lunch counter in the Woolworth drugstore in Greensboro, North Carolina. Within days, similar demonstrations had spread to other cities in North Carolina; within weeks, to surrounding states; and within months, to much of the urban South.

One NAACP official called the demonstrations "the most inspiring, and most dramatic appeals for citizenship of anything I've seen." The sit-ins quickly captured the imagination of the nation, receiving extensive and generally favorable coverage in national newspapers and on television. Leading politicians of both parties, including President Eisenhower and Vice President Nixon, endorsed them. Supportive northerners raised funds to assist jailed southern protestors and conducted their own sympathy demonstrations at local outlets of chain stores whose southern branches discriminated.

Over the next year, southern black youngsters, together with sympathetic whites, "sat in" at restaurants, lunch counters, and libraries; "stood in" at movie theaters; "kneeled in" at churches; and "waded in" at beaches. Protestors were punched by vigilantes, had ketchup poured on their heads, and were burned with lighted cigarettes. All told, an estimated seventy thousand people participated in such demonstrations, and roughly four thousand were arrested. Over a hundred southern localities desegregated some public accommodations as a result.

By the early 1960s, social and political conditions were ripe for racial protest. As southern blacks moved from farms to cities, they organized more easily as a result of superior urban communication and transportation facilities and the growth of black institutions, such as churches and colleges, which provided a framework for social protest. The rising economic status of southern blacks enabled them to finance protest activities and to use economic boycotts to leverage social change. Better education for blacks created leaders who could direct social protest. A better-educated white population meant fewer diehard segregationists.

Greater restraints on violence also facilitated direct-action protest. The increasing political power of northern blacks made the national government more supportive of the civil rights protests of southern blacks. The growing political power of southern blacks made local officeholders more responsive to the concerns of the black community. The explosive growth of national media, especially television, ensured that news of black protest spread quickly to other southern communities, where it could be duplicated, and to the North, where sympathetic audiences rallied in support of its goals.

The ideology of racial equality that suffused World War II left fewer white Americans sympathetic toward Jim Crow. Black soldiers who served during the war were not easily intimidated by the threats of white supremacists, and they often found intolerable the incongruity between their role as soldiers for democracy and their racially subordinate social status.

Conditions for a mass racial protest movement were ripe, but why did the explosion come in 1960 rather than a few years earlier? Two factors may help explain the precise timing of the modern civil rights movement. First, in the 1950s, Americans were preoccupied with the threat of nuclear holocaust and charges of rampant domestic subversion, making the time inopportune for social-reform movements, which were vulnerable to charges of being inspired by Communism. The NAACP devoted considerable energy in the early 1950s to purging left-wingers. By 1960, however, fear of domestic subversion had largely subsided, enabling the emergence of a racial protest movement that was mainly spawned by World War II.

Second, American civil rights leaders identified the freedom movements that erupted across Africa beginning in the late 1950s as an important motivation for their own. The successful efforts of African colonies to win independence demonstrated to American blacks the feasibility of racial change through collective action, while heightening their frustration with the domestic status quo. As black author James Baldwin famously observed, "all of Africa will be free before we can get a lousy cup of coffee."

The increased violence of southern whites against blacks in the late 1950s influenced national opinion on race, but it was neither sufficiently sustained, nor frequently enough captured on television, to generate the widespread outrage that would be necessary to the enactment of transformative civil rights legislation. As of 1960, southern whites still tended to care more about preserving segregation than northern whites did about eliminating it.

In the early 1960s, civil rights leaders evolved a new strategy for turning northern opinion in their favor: they would provoke violence against themselves in settings that were likely to attract national media attention. Because most white Americans in 1960 disapproved of direct-action protest, winning public support required that the protestors be unambiguously in the right and their adversaries in the wrong. Their behavior had to be impeccable and their objectives clearly legitimate.

The success of this strategy also required the "cooperation" of southern law enforcement officers. Peaceful arrests, even if illegal, would dampen protest without generating violent confrontation; the media would get bored, the demonstrators would grow tired, and the federal government would feel no pressure to intervene. By contrast, violent assaults on protestors would capture media attention, outrage northerners, and force government action.

In 1961 the Congress on Racial Equality, counting upon southern racists to create a crisis, sent teams of black and white Freedom Riders into the Deep South to challenge racial segregation in bus station terminals. T. Eugene ("Bull") Connor, the police commissioner of Birmingham, Alabama, happily obliged. Connor was first elected to the Birmingham City Commission in 1937 on a pledge to crush the efforts of national labor unions to organize local steelworkers. But in the early 1950s, civic and political leaders ran him out of politics because they felt that his propensity toward violence against blacks tarnished the city's image and harmed it economically.

In the racial fanaticism that characterized post-*Brown* southern politics, Conner resurrected his political career, regaining his seat on the city commission in 1957 by promising that he would not permit "professional agitators and radicals to come into Birmingham and stir up racial strife." Standing for reelection in 1961, Connor cultivated extremists by offering the Ku Klux Klan fifteen minutes of "open season" on the Freedom Riders as they rolled into town. Promising through an intermediary that he would keep officers away from the scene, Connor reportedly beseeched the Klansmen: "By God, if you are going to do this thing, do it right!" After horrific beatings were administered to the demonstrators, the *Birmingham News* wondered, "Where were the police?" Voters may have been less curious, having handed Connor a landslide victory just two weeks earlier.

When the Freedom Riders traveled on to Montgomery, the police again mysteriously disappeared, and the demonstrators were savagely beaten once more. Governor John Patterson had promised them safe passage, and thus he bore considerable responsibility for the violence. Patterson was one of the South's most extreme segregationist politicians. In the 1958 Alabama gubernatorial race, he had refused to repudiate the endorsement of the Ku Klux Klan. As governor, he warned that southern "enemies" were launching "an all-out war to completely destroy our customs, traditions and way of life." Patterson promised that there would be "hell to pay" if integration were forced on Alabama, and he vowed that when the federal showdown came, "I'll be one of the first ones stirring up trouble, any way I can."

Patterson blamed the Freedom Riders—"professional agitators," he called them—for the violence they had suffered. But national opinion generally deemed him responsible. *Time* wrote that Alabama officials, from "Governor John Patterson on down, abdicated their duties of maintaining law and order." The *Bir-*

mingham News singled out Patterson specifically for blame, noting that he had "talk[ed] for months in a manner that could easily say to the violent, the intemperate ... that they were free to do as they pleased when it came to the hated integrationists."

Alabama politicians had handed the civil rights movement an enormous victory on a silver platter. Reflecting a visceral opposition to direct action, only about 24 percent of Americans had initially supported the Freedom Riders, while 64 percent disapproved. Critics viewed the demonstrators as "provocateurs, or inciters to disorder" and urged them to cease their "exhibition," which was "inflam[ing] ... Southern opinion" and making "advances even more difficult than they already were."

But the Freedom Riders were behaving nonviolently, exercising federally guaranteed rights and enduring vicious beatings. This was southern white supremacy at its ugliest—"the violent brutality of mobsters," as the NAACP described it. Senator Jacob Javits of New York stated that "the whole country must be deeply shocked, appalled and ... ashamed by the ... violence," while Senate Majority Leader Mike Mansfield declared that the Alabama disorders "should cause us—as a nation—to hang our heads in shame." Even in Montgomery and Birmingham, newspapers criticized the "savage scene," the "howling mobs," and the "raging attack." Polls revealed that roughly two-thirds of all Americans now supported the desegregation of public transportation.

In the fall of 1962, when James Meredith integrated the University of Mississippi, the first people were killed in a desegregation riot. Governor Ross Barnett did not openly advocate violence, and he probably hoped to avoid it, but his defiant rhetoric likely contributed to the bloodshed in Oxford, Mississippi.

Barnett was elected governor in 1959 on an extreme segregationist platform. As a candidate, he declared: "Physical courage is

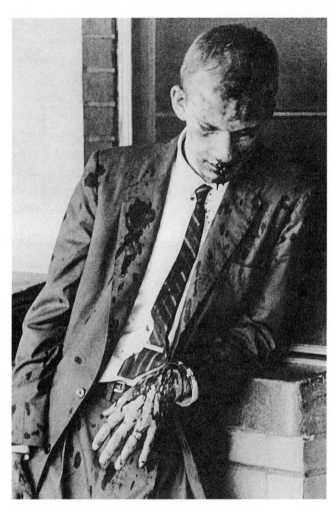

Freedom Rider James Zwerg (1940–), May 20, 1961

a trait sadly lacking in altogether too many of the South's so-called leaders. We must separate the men from the boys. We must identify the traitors in our midst. We must eliminate the cowards from our front lines." In his inaugural address, Barnett promised that "our schools at all levels must be segregated at all costs."

As court-ordered desegregation became imminent at Ole Miss in the summer of 1962, Barnett was trapped. His defiant vows made retreat politically difficult. Rather than preparing Mississippians for the inevitable, he continued to breathe defiance, threatening to arrest federal officers who interfered with state officials performing their duties and calling for the resignation of all state officials who were unwilling to go to jail for defying federal authority.

After twice physically blocking Meredith's entrance to the university, Barnett privately negotiated an agreement with the Justice Department that would enable him to avoid being held in contempt of court by retreating in the face of a public display of federal force. Yet his defiant ravings had created a frenzied atmosphere that Barnett could not control. A race riot involving as many as three thousand people broke out in Oxford on September 30, 1962, killing two and injuring several hundred. Barnett blamed federal marshals for the fiasco, but most national commentators and politicians pinned the responsibility on him.

Beginning late in 1961, the Southern Christian Leadership Conference (SCLC) commenced mass demonstrations against segregation in Albany, Georgia, which lasted for nearly a year. Sheriff Laurie Pritchett peacefully arrested hundreds of demonstrators and outlasted the movement. After Albany, the SCLC's leadership was looking for a city with a police chief who was unlikely to duplicate Pritchett's restraint. They selected Birmingham because of Bull Connor's presence there. Wyatt Walker, an officer of the SCLC, later explained: "We knew that when we came to Birmingham that if Bull Connor was still in control, he would do something to benefit our movement."

In the spring of 1963, their strategy worked brilliantly, as Connor unleashed police dogs and fire hoses against demonstrators, many of whom were children. Television and newspapers featured images of police dogs attacking unresisting demonstrators, including one that President Kennedy reported made him sick. Newspapers called the violence "a national disgrace." Citizens voiced their "sense of unutterable outrage and shame" and demanded that politicians take "action to immediately put to an end the barbarism and savagery in Birmingham." Within ten weeks, spin-off demonstrations had spread to over one hundred cities.

Opinion polls revealed that the percentage of Americans who deemed civil rights to be the nation's most urgent issue rose from 4 percent before Birmingham to 52 percent afterward. President Kennedy now went on national television to announce that civil rights was a "moral issue as old as the scriptures and as clear as the American Constitution," and he radically overhauled his earlier civil rights proposals.

After Kennedy's assassination in November, President Lyndon Johnson told a joint session of Congress that "no memorial oration or eulogy could more eloquently honor President Kennedy's memory than the earliest possible passage of the civil rights bill for which he fought so long." With Johnson's strong backing, the bill became law in the summer of 1964.

In 1964 the civil rights stage shifted back to Mississippi. After struggling for years to organize the state in the face of horrific violence, movement leaders decided to import hundreds of mostly white college students from the North for a "Freedom Summer" of civil rights activity. They understood that bringing "outside agitators" to Mississippi would probably elicit a deadly response, and they calculated that the national media and the Johnson administration would lavish attention on relatively affluent whites from the nation's most prestigious universities.

The strategy worked even more effectively and more tragically than they had anticipated. Within days of their arrival in Mississippi, three civil rights workers—James Chaney, Andrew Goodman, and Michael Schwerner—had disappeared. For much of the summer, FBI agents and the national news media blanketed the state searching for them. Their murders, combined with dozens of church bombings, shootings, beatings, and other atrocities that summer, taught an attentive nation unforgettable lessons about Jim Crow, Mississippi style. The groundwork was laid for further civil rights legislation. Selma brought it to fruition.

Situated in the heart of Alabama's black belt, Selma was home to some of the state's staunchest segregationists and to Jim Clark, sheriff of Dallas County, where Selma is located. One SCLC leader later described Clark as someone who "had grown up believing that in dealing with blacks you could only use billy clubs and guns, since that is all we understood." Early in 1965 the SCLC brought its voter registration campaign to Selma, in search of another Birmingham-style victory.

The result was another resounding success for the civil rights movement. After initially displaying uncharacteristic restraint that disappointed SCLC workers, Clark eventually began brutalizing nonresisting demonstrators. The violence culminated in Bloody Sunday, March 7, 1965, when law enforcement officers viciously assaulted marchers as they crossed the Edmund Pettus Bridge on the way to Montgomery to demonstrate for black enfranchisement.

Governor George Wallace, who was elected in 1962 on a promise to defend segregation "forever," had promised that the march would be broken up by whatever measures were necessary, and his chief law enforcement lieutenant later insisted that the governor himself had given the order to attack. That evening the national television networks broadcast lengthy film reports of peaceful demonstrators being assailed by stampeding horses, flailing clubs, and tear gas. Two white volunteers from the North were killed in the events surrounding Selma, a Unitarian minister from Boston and a mother of five from Detroit.

Most Americans were horrified. *Time* reported that "[r]arely in history has public opinion reacted so spontaneously and with such fury." Huge sympathy demonstrations took place across the nation, and hundreds of clergymen flocked to Selma to show their solidarity with Martin Luther King Jr. and his comrades. Citizens demanded remedial action from their congressional representatives, scores of whom condemned the violence and endorsed voting rights legislation. On March 15, 1965, President Johnson proposed such legislation before a joint session of Congress. Seventy million Americans watched on television as the president beseeched them to "overcome this crippling legacy of bigotry and injustice" and declared his faith that "we shall overcome." That summer the Voting Rights Act became law.

The 1964 Civil Rights Act and the 1965 Voting Rights Act were transformative. At the beginning of the 1963–64 school year, only 1.18 percent of southern black students attended school with whites. The 1964 Act both authorized the U.S. attorney general to bring desegregation suits and provided for the termination of federal education funds for school districts that continued to defy *Brown*. These provisions of the Act, together with aggressive enforcement guidelines issued by the Department of Health, Education, and Welfare, had a dramatic effect: the percentage of southern black children attending school with at least some whites shot up to 6.1 percent in 1966, 16.9 percent in 1967, 32 percent in 1969, and roughly 90 percent in 1973. The 1964 Act also quickly desegregated public accommodations in most of the South.

The 1965 Voting Rights Act proved to be one of the most effective federal statutes in American history. The Act suspended literacy tests for voter registration in most of the South and authorized the appointment of federal registrars to replace state officials in the most recalcitrant southern counties. Before its enactment, only 6.7 percent of age-eligible blacks in Mississippi were registered to vote, and just 23 percent were registered in Alabama. Three years later, black voter registration in both states had climbed to nearly 60 percent. Within a few more years, thousands of blacks had been elected to political office in the South.

As the civil rights movement gained momentum, the Supreme Court issued its most progressive rulings on race. In May 1963, the month that the Birmingham demonstrations culminated in violence, the justices hinted at a new desegregation policy, warning that desegregation plans that "eight years ago might have been deemed sufficient" were no longer so. In June the justices invalidated the same student transfer option that they had declined to review in 1959, observing that the desegregation context had been "significantly altered" since *Brown II*. The next year the Court declared that "[t]he time for mere 'deliberate speed' has run out"; "[t]here has been entirely too much deliberation and not enough speed."

The Court now intervened aggressively in the school desegregation process. In Prince Edward County, Virginia, the public schools were closed in 1959 in response to a federal court's desegregation order. Seventeen hundred black youngsters went largely uneducated for several years. Attorney General Robert Kennedy called the situation "unnatural and unsatisfactory," and it caused the United States international embarrassment. The Johnson administration urged the justices to reopen the schools. In the mid-1950s, there had been much doubt as to whether courts had such authority, as the Constitution does not seem to require states to operate public school systems. In 1964, however, the justices strongly suggested that the county's public schools must be reopened.

In 1968 the Court confronted a desegregation plan under which students were free to choose the school they attended. Under this plan, all whites chose to remain in the "white" school and 85 percent of blacks chose to remain in the "black" school. A decade earlier, the justices probably would have been delighted to sustain such a plan as a good-faith implementation of *Brown,* but now they unanimously invalidated it because of the paltry integration it produced. In 1971 the Court sustained the busing of students to achieve desegregation and approved a sweeping remedial order that neutralized the effects of housing segregation on the racial composition of student bodies. It is safe to say that in 1954 no justice had dreamed of such a thing.

The justices had become fed up with the intransigence of southern whites, and they adjusted legal doctrines accordingly. Exasperated at the bad faith of Alabama jurists, the justices in an unprecedented 1961 decision ordered them to quickly hold a hearing on the NAACP's right to operate in the state or else forfeit jurisdiction to the federal district court. For similar reasons, the Court in 1963 abandoned the traditional requirement that litigants exhaust their state administrative remedies before suing in federal court. In 1964 the Court repudiated an ancient tradition of refusing to inquire into legislative motives and invalidated illicitly motivated school closures. In 1968, because the justices no longer trusted white southerners to do what they were told or to be honest about what they were doing, the Court began to evaluate desegregation plans based on actual results—how many blacks attended mixed schools.

The Court's activism on race extended well beyond the context of school desegregation. Recognizing that only litigation by the NAACP could render *Brown* effective, the justices in a series of decisions created new constitutional law to defend the association from the legal harassment of southern states. The Court ruled that the NAACP did not have to disclose its membership lists, barred states from requiring public school teachers to reveal their organizational affiliations, and overturned a law forbidding organizations from soliciting litigation for their own lawyers. Critics disparagingly referred to the Court as the NAACP's "guardian."

In another series of rulings, the justices turned legal somersaults in order to reverse the criminal convictions of sit-in demonstrators. These cases arose from prosecutions for trespass and breach of the peace of demonstrators seeking to secure desegregation of lunch counters and restaurants in southern states. While refusing to hold that public enforcement of the racially discriminatory preferences of private proprietors was unconstitutional state action, the Court nonetheless reversed convictions in dozens of these cases between 1960 and 1964—mostly on strained rationales.

In other cases as well, the justices stretched to find unconstitutional state action, even going so far as to hold that the repeal by California voters of a legislative fair housing measure was unconstitutional discrimination. The Warren Court also expanded free speech rights to encompass new forms of civil rights protest, created novel procedural rights in an effort to cleanse the criminal justice system of race discrimination, and revolutionized the law of federal courts out of concern that southern state judges would not fairly enforce the constitutional rights of blacks.

During the 1960s, more than in any previous era, the Supreme Court sided with racial minorities against their oppressors. Yet by this date, the justices were following the lead of Congress and the president, who in turn were reflecting a transformation in public opinion on race.

CHAPTER ELEVEN

To the Present

ON AUGUST 29, 2005, Hurricane Katrina, packing winds of 145 miles per hour, slammed into the Gulf Coast just east of New Orleans. The following day, the city's levees broke, the waters rose, and thousands of people climbed onto the roofs of their houses to await rescue—which, for many, never came. Tens of thousands more crammed into the New Orleans Superdome and the Convention Center, where conditions rapidly deteriorated as temperatures rose, toilets stopped working, food and water ran out, and gangs of youths terrorized the occupants. Looting and violence broke out in New Orleans, and dead bodies floated down flooded city streets. More than a thousand people lost their lives in and around the city.

The poor were the hardest hit. They were the ones most likely to live in low-lying neighborhoods and least likely to have cars or other means of escape. They were also disproportionately black. African Americans throughout the nation grew indignant as they watched and waited for someone to rescue the thousands of poor blacks stranded in New Orleans, their lives literally hanging in the balance. More than 80 percent of blacks—but just 20 percent of whites—believed that assistance had been slow to arrive because of the victims' race. Rap star Kanye West declared, "George Bush doesn't care about black people." Most blacks apparently agreed, as the president's approval rating among blacks fell to 2 percent.

Hurricane Katrina was one of the most watched news stories in the last twenty years, and the media framed it around the issues of poverty and race. Americans were forced to confront the plight of the black urban underclass and were appalled by what they saw. The cover story in *Newsweek* was entitled, "An Enduring Shame," and it predicted that the disaster would prompt Americans "to fix their restless gaze on enduring problems of poverty, race and class that have escaped their attention." Senator Barack Obama of Illinois declared: "I hope we realize that the people of New Orleans weren't just abandoned during the hurricane. They were abandoned long ago—to murder and mayhem in the streets, to substandard schools, to dilapidated housing, to inadequate health care, to a pervasive sense of hopelessness."

Commentators predicted that Katrina would launch a "national dialogue on poverty." President Bush went to New Orleans two weeks after the hurricane struck and declared, "Poverty has roots in a history of racial discrimination, which cut off generations from the opportunity of America. We have a duty to confront this poverty with bold action." The president proposed "worker recovery accounts" to help evacuees find work by paying for job training, education, and child care; an Urban Homesteading Act that would donate federal property in the hurricane region for the poor to build homes on; and a Gulf Enterprise Zone to spur business investment in impoverished areas.

The light that Katrina shone on the problems of the black urban underclass quickly dimmed. In 2007 President Bush failed to mention either poverty or Katrina in his State of the Union address, and his proposals for worker recovery accounts and urban homesteading never got off the ground. Many of the poor black residents of New Orleans have yet to recover their pre-hurricane income levels, and they now suffer from increased health problems and their children experience heightened levels of mental health disease.

Despite the gains of the civil rights movement, many blacks today live in entrenched poverty. The failed promise of Hurricane Katrina to revive national interest in the problems of the black urban underclass leaves little reason to be optimistic that solutions will be forthcoming any time soon.

In the mid-1960s, changing social and political conditions slowed racial progress just as the civil rights movement reached its zenith. Even before conditions had changed, though, the movement confronted a significant obstacle: the racial egalitarianism of northern whites had never extended to housing integration. Between 1945 and 1964, efforts by blacks to move into white neighborhoods led to more than a dozen race riots in Chicago alone. In the fall of 1964, as northern voters reelected President Lyndon B. Johnson in a landslide, they simultaneously rejected fair housing laws in several state and local referendums.

In 1966 Martin Luther King Jr. came to Chicago to protest segregated housing. White mobs, carrying signs declaring "Up with Slavery" and "Exterminate the Black Plague," burned cars and threw bricks at blacks marching through working-class ethnic neighborhoods. Many of the white liberals who had applauded the Selma campaign the preceding year now condemned King as irresponsible.

Mayor Richard Daley proved a more formidable adversary to King than had Bull Connor or Jim Clark. He publicly welcomed

Martin Luther King Jr. (1929–1968), assaulted during march in
Chicago, August 5, 1966

King to Chicago, denied that they had conflicting objectives, and
defused the crisis by promising to promote housing integration—
something he had no intention of doing. King's Chicago campaign
was widely judged a disaster, and one of his lieutenants, Hosea
Williams, bleakly concluded, "The Negroes of Chicago have a
greater feeling of powerlessness than any I ever saw.... [T]hey're
beaten down psychologically."

As King's Chicago campaign was imploding, Congress was
killing the Johnson administration's fair housing bill—the first
civil rights measure that would have affected the North as much
as the South. Many northern Democratic congressional representatives who had enthusiastically supported previous civil rights leg-

islation refused to back this measure because of strong opposition in their districts. The House passed a watered-down version of the fair housing bill in July 1966, but even that could not survive a Senate filibuster.

Urban race riots damaged the prospects for fair housing legislation. The first major riot occurred in the Watts neighborhood of Los Angeles in August 1965, just six weeks after President Johnson had signed the Voting Rights Act. Thirty-four people died in the rioting, which caused nearly two hundred million dollars worth of property damage. Similar race riots swept the nation's cities each of the following three summers.

Many blacks saw the rioting as a morally justified response to police brutality and economic exploitation. One black politician observed, "You have to realize the intense pride the Negro in the street felt because of the riots. For once he had made 'the man'... listen to him." By contrast, conservatives tended to blame the riots on "young hoodlums lashing out against society and authority in general" and denied that blacks were "protesting any specific civil rights grievances."

Many white liberals were despondent. One of them observed after Watts: "there were the Negroes—the very people we had loved because they were oppressed—in the role of the aggressor. The mental adjustment was just too much for some white people and we lost them after that." Northern whites proved to be more sympathetic toward well-behaved black children being attacked by white mobs than toward unruly black teenagers yelling "get whitey" and "burn, baby, burn" while looting stores and burning cars. Politicians who took a hard line against the rioters were rewarded at the polls by angry white voters.

Another factor in the unraveling of the civil rights consensus of the mid-1960s was the rise of black nationalism. Its leading promoter, Malcolm X of the Nation of Islam, preached racial pride and self-reliance, denounced nonviolence as cowardly, spoke of whites as "devils," and predicted racial warfare and mass bloodshed. After his assassination in 1965, Malcolm's influence among blacks grew. As one civil rights leader remarked, "Deep in the heart of every black adult lives some of Malcolm and some of King, side by side."

By 1966 black power was superseding integration in some of the leading civil rights organizations. That year Stokely Carmichael assumed leadership of the Student Nonviolent Coordinating Committee (SNCC) and excluded whites from membership while denouncing integration as "a subterfuge for white supremacy." Carmichael told black audiences that he wanted to build "a movement that will smash everything Western civilization has created." His successor as head of SNCC, H. Rap Brown, exhorted blacks to "kill the honkies."

The rise of black power created deep fissures in the civil rights movement. Older leaders, such as Roy Wilkins of the NAACP, denounced black power as "a reverse Mississippi, a reverse Hitler, a reverse Ku Klux Klan." Many whites who were sympathetic to civil rights were appalled by black power, and they terminated financial aid to organizations that preached it.

Even more frightening to most whites was black power's most militant manifestation: the Black Panther Party. The Panthers called for armed self-defense, the killing of racist white police officers, and a black revolution against the white capitalist power structure. After Black Panther founder Huey Newton killed a white police officer in 1967, Panther leaders warned that his execution would take place over their "dead bodies." One Panther declared, "The only thing that's going to free Huey is gunpowder.... How many white people did you kill today?" A national opinion poll revealed that 43 percent of blacks below the age of twenty-one believed that the Panthers represented their political views.

J. Edgar Hoover, the director of the FBI, called the Panthers the greatest threat to the nation's internal security.

By 1966–67 the Vietnam War was also beginning to sap the strength of the civil rights movement. The war diverted national attention from issues of racial equality. From the summer of 1963 through the spring of 1965, Americans ranked civil rights as the nation's leading issue, but then the war in Vietnam displaced it.

The war also divided the civil rights movement. In 1966 SNCC came out in opposition to the war, and the following year, so did King and the SCLC. King urged blacks to become conscientious objectors, reasoning that a nonviolent protest movement could not support the United States becoming "the greatest purveyor of violence in the world today." He also protested that "Negroes and poor people generally are bearing the heaviest burden of this war." King denounced the war as "a blasphemy against all that America stands for" and accused American military forces of "committing atrocities equal to any perpetrated by the Vietcong."

Such comments caused a national hullabaloo. The *New York Times* predicted "disastrous" consequences from uniting the peace movement with the civil rights movement, and the NAACP agreed that King had made "a serious tactical mistake." Senator Barry Goldwater of Arizona went further, suggesting that King's comments "could border a bit on treason."

The challenge to northern housing segregation, urban race riots, the rise of black power, and growing opposition to the Vietnam War accelerated a national political realignment that was already underway. In 1964 the Republican Party nominated as its presidential candidate Senator Goldwater, who was a staunch opponent of the Johnson administration's civil rights bill. Although Goldwater suffered a landslide defeat, he did win (in addition to his home state of Arizona) the five states of the Deep South, which had not voted Republican since Reconstruction, as well as a majority of the white vote in several other southern states.

By 1966 the racial backlash was spreading to the North. In September an opinion poll revealed that 52 percent of respondents—double the number of the preceding year—believed that the Johnson administration was pushing too aggressively for civil rights. One White House aide told President Johnson, "White people are scared and sore and the consensus behind improvement of the Negro's condition is running out—has run out." Journalists began to predict a white voter backlash and to draw analogies to the collapse of northern white support for Reconstruction in the mid-1870s. In November Democrats lost forty-nine seats in the House, and a movie actor named Ronald Reagan rode the white backlash to victory in the California gubernatorial election.

Two years later, Republican Richard M. Nixon won the presidency on a platform emphasizing law and order, a relaxed pace for school desegregation in the South, and opposition to busing. Nixon declared during the campaign, "I don't believe you should use the South as a whipping boy," and he warned that when children were bused "into a strange community ... you destroy that child." Ninety-seven percent of blacks voted for Democrat Hubert Humphrey that year, but only 35 percent of whites did so. The 14 percent of voters who supported George Wallace's third-party bid for the presidency encouraged the Republican Party to become even more conservative on race issues in the future.

Nixon's victory at the polls translated directly into changes in the Court's racial jurisprudence: he appointed four new justices during his first term. In its initial rulings on school desegregation, however, the Burger Court, named for Chief Justice Warren Burger, continued to act aggressively. When the Court declared in

1969 that desegregation extensions would no longer be granted to school districts, Nixon privately raged at "the Court's naive stupidity," and he denounced the justices as "irresponsible... clowns."

In 1971 the justices unanimously sustained student busing as a remedy for segregation, and they approved the imposition of sweeping desegregation orders upon proof of fairly minimal constitutional violations. When the justices confronted their first northern school desegregation case in 1973, however, they could not agree on how to handle school segregation that resulted primarily from segregated housing patterns.

In 1974 the Court decided its most important school desegregation case since *Brown*. In *Milliken v. Bradley*, by a five-to-four vote, the justices barred the inclusion of largely white suburbs within an urban school desegregation decree, absent proof that school district lines had been racially gerrymandered. As a result, federal courts were disabled from accomplishing meaningful school desegregation in most cities. Nixon's appointees comprised four of the five justices in the majority.

The *Milliken* ruling reflected growing public hostility toward school desegregation. When northern whites had regarded school segregation as a southern problem, they agreed it must end. As school desegregation litigation migrated northwards, however, northern whites began demanding congressional action against busing. In 1972 Congress prohibited the use of federal funds for busing that was intended to achieve racial balance, and in 1974, it prohibited federal courts from requiring busing to remedy segregation that was not attributable to state action.

A few months after *Milliken*, Boston erupted in antibusing riots. Blacks being transported into heavily Irish Catholic South Boston were greeted with rocks and bottles. Black youngsters in Roxbury retaliated by stoning passing cars and beating a white cab driver.

According to the *New York Times*, many southerners "saw a fine irony in the fact that Boston, the seat of the abolitionist movement and the very symbol of Eastern liberalism," should find it so difficult to accept school integration.

For the next fifteen years, the Court narrowly sustained broad desegregation remedies *within* cities, while rejecting decrees that included the suburbs and warning lower court judges not to use school desegregation orders to undo the effects of segregated housing. A series of conservative Court appointments by Presidents Ronald Reagan and George H. W. Bush between 1986 and 1991 altered this status quo.

In a case from Oklahoma City in 1991, a narrowly divided Court ruled that once a school board had complied in good faith for a "reasonable period of time" with a desegregation order, and the vestiges of past discrimination had been eliminated "to the extent practicable," the school district was entitled to be released from federal supervision. If terminating a desegregation decree under these conditions resulted in increased school segregation, then private housing preferences were probably the cause, and the state bore no responsibility for them. In short, the conservative majority's patience for court-ordered school desegregation had run out. So had public support. An opinion poll conducted around this time revealed that 93 percent of whites supported school integration in principle, but just 26 percent favored government intervention to accomplish it.

In 1995 the conservative justices indicated that their tolerance for remedial alternatives to busing had also worn thin. In a five-to-four decision, the conservative majority forbade the use of magnet school programs for the purpose of enticing suburban whites into racially integrated urban schools and imposed virtually insurmountable hurdles to judicially mandated increases in educational funding as a remedy for school segregation.

By the early twenty-first century, court-ordered desegregation was winding down, as dozens of districts were being released from federal desegregation decrees. In 2006–07, the Supreme Court was asked to forbid school districts from *voluntarily* promoting integration through race-conscious student assignment policies.

One of the most crucial racial issues confronting the Burger Court was whether laws that made no mention of race but adversely impacted a minority group were unconstitutional, or whether a discriminatory purpose also had to be shown in order to invalidate them. In *Washington v. Davis* (1976), the Court ruled that the Equal Protection Clause required proof of illicit motivation. Even though blacks were four times as likely as whites to fail an aptitude test to become a police officer, the test was constitutionally permissible so long as it had not been adopted for the purpose of disadvantaging blacks.

The issue in *Washington v. Davis* is genuinely difficult. To invalidate all laws that produce racially disparate effects would require government officials constantly to consider race and would jeopardize all legislation that disproportionately burdens the poor, given the strong correlation between minority racial status and poverty. Yet to sustain such laws is to allow government to compound the disadvantages of historically oppressed racial minorities without good reason and to permit much legislation that was invidiously motivated to pass constitutional muster, given the difficulty of proving intentional race discrimination. Conservative and liberal justices differed in how to strike the balance between such considerations.

The controversy over how to punish the possession and sale of crack and powder cocaine illustrates the practical consequences of *Washington v. Davis*. In the midst of media hysteria over a rising crack epidemic, Congress in 1986 dramatically increased punishments: a defendant convicted of possessing five grams of crack would receive the same prison sentence as one possessing five hundred grams of powder cocaine. Because crack is more addictive and produces a more volatile high, some punishment differential seems justified. But because 90 percent of federal crack defendants—and only 25 percent of powder defendants—are black, the punishment differential has an enormous racially disparate impact. Under *Washington v. Davis*, however, lower courts have generally rejected equal protection challenges to this disparity.

In the last thirty years, the Court has struggled with another important race issue: affirmative action. In 1978, by a five-to-four vote, the Court invalidated the affirmative action policy of the University of California at Davis Medical School, which set aside sixteen slots in a class of one hundred for members of minority racial groups. In this and subsequent decisions, conservative justices objected to affirmative action as unfair to innocent whites and inconsistent with the Fourteenth Amendment's philosophy of government color-blindness. Liberals noted the irony of using this amendment, which was adopted to protect African Americans from discrimination, to invalidate legislation that was designed to benefit them. Liberals also observed that for nearly one hundred years, courts had permitted racial classifications under the Equal Protection Clause; only when those classifications were first used to benefit blacks did courts begin to insist on government color-blindness.

The justices were narrowly divided on affirmative action, sustaining some plans and invalidating others, until the appointment of several conservatives between 1986 and 1991 produced a reliable five-person majority to invalidate most such policies. The conservative majority ruled that all racial classifications—whether their intent was benign or malign—must be subjected to the same exacting judicial scrutiny. They insisted on specific proof of the past discrimination that affirmative action policies purported to remedy, and they required that minority racial preferences, in order to survive constitutional scrutiny, be scrupulously structured to benefit only those who were themselves victimized by past discrimination and to avoid burdening too many innocents. Under these standards, most affirmative action plans were unconstitutional.

In a related series of five-to-four rulings, the Court struck down several congressional districts that had been gerrymandered to enhance the prospects of minority racial groups electing representatives of their own race. The conservative justices ruled that the Fourteenth Amendment generally forbids such districts—even though the amendment's purpose had been to protect only civil rights, not political rights.

Because most of the Court's recent race rulings were five to four, the shift of a single justice could change outcomes. Early in the twenty-first century, Justice Sandra Day O'Connor switched sides, producing five-to-four victories for the liberals in two important cases. In the first, she joined an opinion sustaining a congressional district that had been gerrymandered to produce a black representative. In the second, she wrote the majority opinion sustaining the race-conscious admissions policy of the University of Michigan School of Law.

Changes in public opinion and O'Connor's reluctance to disrupt the racial status quo may explain her shift. Reflecting the nation's growing racial diversity and the forces of globalization, most Americans had come to expect important social, political, and economic institutions to "look like America." Friend-of-the-court briefs filed in the University of Michigan case revealed that even relatively conservative institutions, such as Fortune 500 companies and the U.S. military, had embraced a multiracial vision, warning the justices that America's economic success and military strength depended on the continued use of affirmative action. Justice O'Connor proved receptive to such appeals.

As the Court became more conservative in the late twentieth century, its rulings manifested less concern with race discrimination in the criminal justice system. In *McCleskey v. Kemp* (1987), the Court confronted an equal-protection challenge to the discriminatory administration of the death penalty in Georgia. According to a study that the justices accepted as valid, defendants who murdered whites were 4.3 times more likely to receive the death penalty than were those who murdered blacks.

Rejecting the challenge by a five-to-four vote, the Court observed that so long as actors administering the death penalty—such as prosecutors and jurors—exercised significant discretion, eliminating race discrimination entirely was impossible. The majority also noted that, given similar racial disparities throughout the criminal justice system, vindicating McCleskey's claim would have had potentially enormous consequences. McCleskey was eventually executed; had he killed a black man, he almost certainly would not have been.

In a 1996 decision, the Court imposed a virtually insurmountable hurdle for defendants who alleged racially selective prosecution. Before black defendants could gain access to the prosecutor's files to corroborate such claims, they had to demonstrate that similarly situated whites had not been prosecuted. This was a Catch 22: how could black defendants show that similarly situated whites had not been prosecuted without access to the prosecutor's files?

The Court refused to assume that all races are equally likely to commit all crimes. Thus, it denied that this U.S. attorney's prosecution of twenty-four blacks and no whites for crack distribution in the preceding year was significant evidence of selective prosecution. The vote was eight-to-one, suggesting that even the liberal justices were no longer terribly concerned about race discrimination in the criminal justice system.

In the last half century, America has experienced revolutionary racial change. Racially motivated lynchings and state-sponsored racial segregation have been largely eradicated. Public accommodations and places of employment have been integrated to a significant degree.

Today blacks register to vote in roughly the same percentages as whites, and the number of black elected officials has skyrocketed. Most major cities with large black populations have elected black mayors. Blacks, who constitute 11.3 percent of the nation's voting-age population, make up 9.7 percent of the House of Representatives. More than nine thousand blacks now hold elected office.

Blacks also occupy some of the U.S. government's most important nonelective positions. Since 1967 a black man—first Thurgood Marshall, then Clarence Thomas—has sat on the Supreme Court. The first black federal judge was appointed in the late 1930s; today blacks constitute 11 percent of the federal judiciary. In 1989 Colin Powell became the first black chairman of the Joint Chiefs of Staff. No blacks sat in the president's Cabinet until 1966; the last two secretaries of state, the highest ranking Cabinet officer, have been black.

Blacks have made dramatic gains in education and employment. The difference in the median number of school years completed by blacks and whites fell from 3.5 in 1954 to 0.4 in 1972. The number of blacks attending college increased 500 percent between 1960 and 1977. The number of blacks holding white-collar or middle-class jobs increased from 12.1 percent in 1960 to

30.4 percent in 1990. By the late 1970s, black men with college degrees earned 93 percent as much as their white counterparts.

Yet many racial barriers remain. As late as 1990, only one black in the House represented a majority-white constituency. There have been only three black U.S. senators since Reconstruction and even fewer black governors. While most major cities have had black mayors, their ability to improve the lives of minority citizens is severely handicapped by industrial decline, shrinking tax bases, and rising crime rates. Since 1980 national politics has been largely dominated by a Republican Party that rarely captures as much as 10 percent of the black vote in presidential elections and has consistently opposed affirmative action and efforts to promote integration in housing and education.

As late as 1998, not a single Fortune 1000 company had a black chief executive officer. Blacks also remain severely underrepresented in professions such as law, medicine, and engineering. A 1990 study found that only 1 percent of the partners in the nation's 250 largest law firms were black.

American culture today celebrates the ideals of racial equality and integration. Some black athletes and entertainers are cultural icons. Promotional literature from universities and corporations are replete with images of racially integrated student bodies and workforces. Popular television programs—and the less popular advertisements that permeate them—usually have racially diverse casts. The dominant culture strongly condemns and penalizes open displays of racism. In 2002 Trent Lott of Mississippi had to resign as Senate majority leader after stating at a party celebrating the one hundredth birthday of Senator Strom Thurmond that the country might have been better off had Thurmond won his 1948 presidential bid—when he ran as the candidate of the openly white supremacist Dixiecrats.

Yet progress toward genuine racial integration has almost completely stalled. Housing segregation has increased dramatically in the last fifty years, as whites have fled cities for surrounding suburbs, and systemic racial discrimination in housing markets has generally prevented blacks from following. Among ethnic and racial groups in American history, only blacks have continued to experience the same rates of residential segregation across generations. In recent decades, middle-class blacks have also fled cities for suburbs. Yet black suburbanization has had little effect on residential segregation, as a large influx of even middle-class blacks tends to drive whites away.

Because most children attend schools in their neighborhoods, housing segregation almost inevitably means school segregation. Outside of the South, schools in most of the nation's large cities are more segregated today than they were in 1954. Most of those whites who have remained in cities have fled public schools for private ones. Whites were 33 percent of the public school population of New Orleans in 1968, but only 8 percent in 1993.

Ironically, the South today has the most racially integrated schools in the nation. Yet even in the South, school integration has been declining since the 1970s, partly because courts have been terminating desegregation decrees. Moreover, students in integrated schools are generally tracked in ways that highly correlate with race, so that individual classrooms remain overwhelmingly segregated. Blacks and whites attending the same schools also tend to eat at different tables in the cafeteria, use different bathroom facilities, and participate in different sports.

In the South, three out of five blacks attending college choose historically black institutions, while the large state universities remain overwhelmingly white. As one black student recently explained, "I have to deal with racism the rest of my life. Why should I deal with that in college?"

For the most part, blacks and whites attend different churches, listen to different radio stations, and socialize in different venues. Americans spend an average of seven hours a day watching television, but media markets have grown increasingly segregated by race. In 1996–97, only one of the top twenty television shows among black households—*Monday Night Football*—was in the top twenty for whites. Relatively few blacks watched the enormously popular situation comedies *Friends* and *Seinfeld*. The shows that whites tend to watch—especially local news programs—have more racially diverse casts than most whites experience in their daily lives, thus creating an illusory "virtual integration" that causes whites to underestimate how segregated American society remains. Magazine readership is also stunningly segregated: in a typical month, half of all blacks read *Ebony*, while fewer than one in every hundred whites does so.

The workplace is supposedly the most integrated sphere of American life, but interactions there are usually better characterized as racial "intersection" than "integration." Large corporations that claim to prize diversity often place blacks in positions with high public profiles but relatively little decision-making authority. In the National Basketball Association, for example, blacks comprise half of all community relations directors but less than 10 percent of team vice presidents. Many companies hire just enough blacks to insulate themselves from discrimination lawsuits or consumer boycotts. Black executives and professionals are still sufficiently rare in most corporations that they are routinely mistaken for file clerks, messengers, or secretaries.

Even American sports are segregated to an astonishing degree. Baseball, which Jackie Robinson desegregated in 1947, is losing both black participation and black audiences. Some historically black colleges have recently abandoned baseball for lack of interest. Ice hockey, tennis, and golf have notoriously little black participation. Track and field, which is well integrated, tends to segregate according to whether a particular event emphasizes speed or endurance.

On its surface, the National Football League seems very well integrated: two-thirds of the players are black, and one-third is white. Yet in 1995, blacks were just 9 percent of professional quarterbacks, while they were 90 percent of running backs and wide receivers, and 100 percent of defensive cornerbacks. Whites are represented disproportionately on the offensive line, where intelligence is prized, and blacks on the defensive line, where greater emphasis is placed on athleticism.

Middle-class blacks face far more overt race *discrimination* than most whites care to acknowledge. Deval Patrick, who recently became only the second black governor in American history, had difficulty hailing cabs after White House meetings with President Bill Clinton when he served as assistant attorney general. Security personnel in high-end stores routinely shadow black shoppers. Several leading restaurant chains have recently admitted to discriminating against black customers. State highway patrols routinely engage in racial profiling, and many black superstar athletes have given up their fancy cars after repeatedly being stopped and harassed by suspicious police officers.

No matter how wealthy or accomplished, blacks regularly have to suffer such indignities. Even worse, they have to endure whites telling them that racial bigotry is mainly a thing of the past, while their everyday experiences indicate otherwise. No wonder that so many blacks have grown disillusioned with integration.

For the African American underclass, the situation is much bleaker and growing worse. In 1990 nearly two-thirds of black children were born outside of marriage, compared with just 15 percent of white children. Well over half of black families were headed by single mothers. In 2004 nearly 25 percent of blacks—three times the percentage of whites—lived in poverty. That racial gap has narrowed little over the past three decades.

The unemployment rate for blacks has historically averaged twice that for whites. Racially discriminatory barriers to high-paying manufacturing jobs were dismantled just as those jobs began to disappear as a result of technological advances and international competition. In 1990 the average family income for blacks was still just 58 percent of that for whites. Racial disparities in wealth are staggering. The average black family has only about 10 percent of the wealth of the average white family—making it much harder for blacks to set up their own businesses.

Racial segregation in housing compounds the problems of the black urban underclass. Because American cities are more racially segregated than economically segregated, and because blacks are poorer than whites, black neighborhoods are characterized by concentrated poverty. They are likely to have dilapidated housing, poor schools, broken families, juvenile pregnancies, drug dependency, high crime rates, and a lack of positive role models for youngsters. The percentage of blacks living in neighborhoods of extreme poverty increased dramatically between 1970 and 1990.

Spatial segregation means social isolation, as most inner-city blacks are rarely exposed to whites or the broader culture. As a result, black youngsters have developed a separate language of sorts, which disadvantages them in school and in the search for employment. Even worse, social segregation has fostered an oppositional culture among many black youngsters that discourages academic achievement—"acting white"—and thus further disables them from succeeding in mainstream society.

The pathologies of the black urban underclass are so severe today that more black men are incarcerated than are attending college. Blacks comprise less than 12 percent of the nation's population but more than 50 percent of its prison inmates and roughly 48 percent of those on death row. Black men are seven times more likely to be incarcerated than white men.

The nation's racial demographics are becoming increasingly complex. The Latino population doubled between 1970 and 1990, and Latinos recently surpassed blacks as the nation's largest racial minority. The Asian population tripled from 1.3 percent to 3.8 percent during the same period. The nation's largest state, California, is no longer majority white, and the country as a whole will probably cease to be so in the middle of the twenty-first century.

Yet Asians and Latinos are assimilating into mainstream society much more quickly than are blacks. Neither group is as residentially segregated as are blacks. The most affluent blacks are more residentially segregated than the poorest Hispanics in Los Angeles and the poorest Asians in San Francisco. Intermarriage rates also differ vastly across these minority groups: for blacks, it is only 6 percent, while it is 35 percent for native-born Hispanics and 50 percent for native-born Asians.

The growing success and assimilation of other racial minorities highlights the extent to which some African Americans remain isolated and impoverished. For many blacks, the goals of equality and racial integration are as distant today as they have ever been.

Conclusion

. . .

DESPITE THE CONTINUED EXISTENCE of a racially defined urban underclass, America has undeniably made great progress toward racial equality. Slavery, lynching, race-based disfranchisement, and state-mandated segregation have all been eliminated and are unlikely to return.

Racial progress has been episodic rather than ineluctable. Northern blacks were better treated legally in 1810 than in 1860. Southern blacks voted, served on juries, and held public office in 1870 but not in 1910. Northern blacks were more likely to attend racially integrated schools and live in racially integrated neighborhoods in 1910 than in 1930.

The rights of blacks have repeatedly been subordinated to the interests of others. In *Prigg v. Pennsylvania* (1842), the Supreme Court privileged the right of southern masters to recover their fugitive slaves over the interest of northern free blacks in avoiding kidnapping and enslavement. In 1876–77, the Republican Party sacrificed the rights of southern blacks in order to secure the presidency. In the 1930s President Franklin D. Roosevelt refused to support an antilynching bill for fear of alienating southern Democrats whose support he needed to enact New Deal legislation.

Racial progress has rarely been a result of people simply doing the right thing. The Constitution's framers authorized future congressional restrictions on the foreign slave trade mainly because Virginians and Marylanders had more slaves than they needed and wanted to keep the price of slaves high. During Reconstruction, Republicans enfranchised blacks largely because they anticipated that blacks would vote for them. The Truman and Eisenhower administrations supported civil rights principally in order to secure black votes and deprive the Soviet Union of valuable propaganda opportunities.

Blacks have had to fight for every inch of racial progress. Slave escapes and revolts increased the anxiety of southern masters, leading them to demand greater protections for slavery from the federal government, which northerners eventually tired of providing. Between 1910 and 1960, millions of southern blacks migrated to northern cities in search of better jobs and more dignified treatment, eventually producing a dramatic shift in the national politics of civil rights. In 1941 a threatened march on Washington, D.C., by one hundred thousand blacks induced President Roosevelt to issue an executive order banning race discrimination in defense industries.

Black activism alone has been insufficient to generate progressive racial change; auspicious social and political conditions have also been necessary. Ironically, wars have generally advanced the cause of racial equality. The Revolutionary War temporarily weakened slavery in the South and enabled its gradual abolition in the North. The Civil War emancipated slaves and inspired postwar constitutional amendments protecting the civil and political rights of blacks. Black membership in the NAACP increased tenfold during World War I, and World War II helped launch the modern civil rights movement.

Several factors account for wars' racially egalitarian influence. Americans tend to define their war aims in democratic terms. The purpose of World War I was "to make the world safe for democracy," and the goal of World War II was to defeat fascism. The democratic ideologies of these wars forced Americans to confront— and to partially reform—undemocratic practices such as racial subordination. Wars also disrupt traditional patterns of status and behavior. Lincoln was driven to emancipate and then arm the slaves after a yearlong effort at suppressing disunionism without challenging prevailing racial norms had proved unavailing. Finally, wars usually involve common sacrifice for the general good and thus have inescapably egalitarian implications. Thus, the sacrifices of liberated slaves on Civil War battlefields paved the way for black enfranchisement.

Long-term forces such as urbanization, improved education, and technological advances have also fostered progressive racial change. Urban blacks commanded greater economic resources, which allowed them to fund social protest, dramatized the disparities between their economic and social statuses, and enabled them to use economic boycotts to leverage social change. Urban blacks created institutions, such as churches and colleges, which helped to organize and lead social protest; better urban transportation and communication also facilitated such protest.

Cities, even in the South, tended to have more permissive racial mores. Urban blacks found it easier to vote, and they used their political influence to obtain the physical security that enabled social protest. By the 1940s most southern cities had NAACP branches, which shared information about racial conditions elsewhere, offered legal expertise for challenging rights violations, and spread the risks and the costs of racial protest.

Better education for blacks encouraged them to challenge their subordinate social status, made it harder for whites to justify that status, and facilitated the coordination of social protest. Improved education for whites reduced their commitment to the harshest aspects of Jim Crow.

As the South became less insular, whites found racial change harder to resist. World War II introduced millions of southerners, white and black, to novel racial attitudes and practices. The growth of the mass media exposed millions more to outside influences, while undermining the ability of white southerners to restrict outside scrutiny of their treatment of blacks.

Shifting political coalitions have also influenced racial change. In the 1890s, as Republicans discovered that they could control the national government without southern electoral support, they lost their enthusiasm for protecting the voting rights of southern blacks. During the Great Depression, blacks regained national political influence by dividing their votes between the major political parties at the same moment that many northern states became electorally competitive for the first time in generations. One recent impediment to progressive racial change has been the tendency of blacks to vote overwhelmingly Democratic at a time when Republicans have generally dominated national politics.

International developments have affected domestic racial policies. The decolonization of Africa around 1960 inspired American blacks to demand their constitutional rights. During the cold war, competition with the Soviet Union for the allegiance of nonwhite developing nations forced Americans to reform domestic racial practices in order to prove that democratic capitalism was not synonymous with white supremacy.

Improved physical security for southern blacks has been critical to progressive racial change. In 1919 whites in Texas could maim the NAACP's national secretary in broad daylight and go unpunished. A southern civil rights movement was almost in-conceivable in such an environment, and even litigation chal-lenging racial injustice was difficult to sustain. In the 1960s, by contrast, southern civil rights demonstrators could generally en-gage in direct-action protest without risking deadly physical violence.

Ironically, the relative decline in white-on-black violence, which made civil rights protest possible, ensured that any residual violence would stand out. White southerners lynched a hundred blacks a year around 1900, yet most northerners showed little concern. In the 1960s, however, law enforcement brutalization of peaceful protestors was piped directly into American homes by television, shocking northerners and leading directly to the enact-ment of civil rights legislation.

Because southern whites staunchly resisted progressive racial change, pressure was required to bring it about. Southern blacks supplied some of that pressure, yet the system of white suprem-acy was so ruthless and pervasive that internally generated change was difficult to accomplish. Because southern whites did not permit blacks to become very well educated, there were few black lawyers available to challenge the system in court, and most white lawyers refused to take civil rights cases. Southern blacks could not vote, making political reform of white supremacy virtually impossible. Because whites controlled the livelihood of most blacks, racial protest usually resulted in severe economic reprisals. The threat and reality of physical violence ultimately secured the system against most internal challenges.

Only external pressure could change such a system. Northern-ers fought a civil war to end slavery, and during Reconstruction, the northern-dominated Republican Party temporarily revolution-ized southern race relations. In the twentieth century, external pressure was supplied first by the NAACP and later by northern public opinion and the national government.

The NAACP's lobbying campaign for federal antilynching legislation induced southern states to take action against lynching. The NAACP's litigation campaigns prompted southern states to begin equalizing spending on black education and permitting blacks to register to vote. Pressure from the national government helped create a relatively secure physical environment for southern black protest. Ultimately, civil rights legislation supplied coercive mechanisms that accelerated the downfall of southern Jim Crow.

To be sure, the North was never a bastion of racial equality. Slavery was entrenched in most northern colonies before the Revolutionary War. Jacksonian Democrats in the North proclaimed the equality of all white men while disfranchising blacks, segregating them, and trying to colonize them overseas. After World War I, northern blacks who sought to purchase homes in white neighborhoods frequently encountered howling mobs, burning crosses, and bombs. Martin Luther King Jr.'s greatest defeat came in Chicago, where he unsuccessfully challenged housing segregation in 1966.

Still, the North has usually been more racially tolerant than the South, and this regional variation has driven progressive racial change. Had the North not abandoned slavery, no Civil War would have occurred. Had blacks not been permitted to vote in the North after 1870, the Great Migration could not have enhanced black political power and induced the national government to support civil rights. The NAACP's ability to challenge southern racial practices depended on the relative freedom of northern blacks to organize racial protest.

Much of the racial change driven by regional variation has been unintended. The North went to war against the South in

1861 to suppress disunionism but ended up abolishing slavery as well. During Reconstruction, northern Republicans enacted the Fifteenth Amendment primarily to establish a southern political base, but one of the amendment's most important long-term consequences was the political empowerment of northern blacks following the Great Migration. In *Brown v. Board of Education*, a Supreme Court with a northern majority sought to end southern Jim Crow, but ended up radicalizing southern politics, creating an environment ripe for violence, and ultimately facilitating the enactment of transformative civil rights legislation.

Regional differences in racial mores have created a dynamic that has regularly promoted progressive racial change: anxious and defensive white southerners have taken actions to preserve white supremacy that have impelled northerners to assail it. Increasingly strident northern denunciations of slavery induced anxious southern slave owners to demand and receive slavery guarantees from the federal government, which alienated many northerners, who feared a "slave power conspiracy" to deprive them of their liberties. After World War II, a crescendo of southern white violence aimed at suppressing black civil rights militancy inspired President Truman to appoint a civil rights committee which recommended progressive racial reforms. The massive resistance of southern whites to *Brown* eventually drove the Supreme Court to embrace increasingly egalitarian interpretations of the Constitution. The harder southern whites fought to preserve white supremacy, the more they accelerated its demise.

Law has played an ambiguous role in the history of American racial equality. The law on the books has frequently borne little relationship to the law in action. Many slaves became literate despite legal prohibitions on teaching slaves to read and write. In the 1850s blacks continued to enter those states that had constitutionally barred their admission. Miscegenation bans did not prevent the formation of interracial couples.

Civil rights legislation was often no more consequential. The 1875 Civil Rights Act was a dead letter before the Supreme Court struck it down, and so were the many northern public accommodations laws adopted soon thereafter. In 1875 Congress barred race discrimination in jury selection, but by 1910 blacks were no longer sitting on southern juries. Although southern state constitutions required the equal funding of black schools, enormous racial disparities in educational spending developed after 1900, and they were almost never challenged in court.

Not only was legislation often powerless to undermine white supremacy; it was also usually unnecessary to sustain it. No northern state mandated residential segregation by law, yet northern blacks lived in pervasively segregated neighborhoods. Before World War I, northern blacks were almost universally excluded from decent industrial jobs, even though no law commanded racial discrimination in employment. Most southern railroads segregated their passengers before states enacted compulsory segregation laws. Southern statutes did not require that blacks give way to whites on public sidewalks or refer to whites by courtesy titles, yet blacks failing to do so acted at their peril.

Jim Crow laws were often enacted for symbolic reasons, not functional ones. When Kentucky in 1904 passed a law requiring segregation in education, only one school in the state was racially integrated—and it was barely so. Texas adopted a law excluding blacks from party primaries in order to suppress a handful of renegade counties that permitted blacks to participate.

In other contexts, however, law proved vital to both the creation and the destruction of white supremacy. Voter registration requirements adopted around 1890 disfranchised enough southern blacks and their sympathizers to enable a wholesale assault on black suffrage. Southern utility companies would not have segregated their streetcars early in the twentieth century without legal compulsion. The 1964 Civil Rights Act was critical to the desegregation of southern schools and public accommodations, and the 1965 Voting Rights Act revolutionized black voter registration in the Deep South.

The Supreme Court's contributions to racial equality have also been ambiguous. In the nineteenth century, the Court was a consistent foe of racial minorities. The justices invalidated a northern state's effort to protect free blacks from kidnapping by slave catchers, voided a congressional ban on slavery in the federal territories, denied that free blacks possessed any rights "which the white man was bound to respect," freed the perpetrators of white-on-black lynchings and racial massacres, invalidated a federal public accommodations law, and upheld most of the anti-Chinese measures enacted by state and federal governments.

Well into the twentieth century, the Court sustained the constitutionality of racial segregation and black disfranchisement, and during World War II, it upheld the Japanese American internment. More recently, the justices have invalidated affirmative action plans and legislative schemes designed to promote minority political representation. On the other side of the balance sheet, beginning in the 1910s, the Court gradually eliminated southern schemes for disfranchising blacks, curbed the legal lynching of black criminal defendants, and eventually invalidated racial segregation in housing, transportation, and public education.

This historical performance suggests that the Court has hardly been an unvarnished defender of the rights of racial minorities. The justices reflect dominant public opinion too much for them to protect truly oppressed groups. That anyone should believe otherwise is probably attributable to *Brown* and its progeny. Yet those rulings reflected social and political change at least as much as they caused them. The justices who decided *Brown* understood this, commenting on the "spectacular" advances and the "constant progress" already being made in race relations. Such changes were sufficient to overcome what several of the justices considered a weak legal case for invalidating school segregation.

Constitutional rights do not matter much unless they are enforced. Even when the Court has issued racially progressive rulings, they have often proved inefficacious. *Buchanan v. Warley* (1917) did not integrate neighborhoods, and for ten years, *Brown* was almost completely nullified in the Deep South. Other decisions have been much more consequential. *Sweatt v. Painter* (1950) integrated public universities outside of the Deep South, and *Smith v. Allwright* (1944) inspired a revolution in black voter registration in southern cities. Which political and social conditions have influenced the efficacy of the Court's progressive race rulings?

One reason that *Smith* was more immediately efficacious than *Brown* is that all blacks thought they should be allowed to vote, but some blacks preferred equally funded but racially separate schools to integrated ones. In addition, the democratic ideology of World War II more directly implicated the right to vote than the right to nonsegregated education. Black soldiers returning to the South after the war often took their discharge papers straight to city hall to register to vote; they did not proceed directly to local school boards to demand integrated education for their children.

Blacks were more divided over some rights than others, but they were more militant about enforcing all rights after World War II than before. This greater militancy was partly a product of greater physical security. Constitutional rights are not worth much when asserting them is likely to get one beaten or killed. Southern railroads would likely have remained segregated even had *Plessy* been decided differently, because blacks testing a right to non-segregated travel would have jeopardized their lives in an era of rampant lynching. By 1950, however, lynchings were nearly obsolete, and postwar black litigants were far more likely to face economical reprisals than physical violence.

The intensity of opponents' resistance also influenced the efficacy of the Court's progressive race rulings. By the 1940s most southern whites were less resistant to black suffrage than they were to integrated grade school education. The democratic ideology of World War II and advances in black education led many southern whites to conclude that white primaries were a "cruel and shameful thing." By contrast, most white southerners continued to fiercely resist grade school desegregation, which involved the race mixing of young children, male and female, and thus for most whites had inevitable connotations of miscegenation.

The public enforcement of civil rights was, unsurprisingly, more effective than private enforcement. The Justice Department commanded far greater resources than did the NAACP; it monopolized criminal enforcement; and it did not bear the same risks of economic reprisals and physical retaliation. One reason that *Smith* proved so efficacious is that the Justice Department made credible threats to enforce it. Similarly, the pace of school desegregation accelerated dramatically after the 1964 Civil Rights Act authorized lawsuits by the attorney general. Public enforcement also offers remedial options that are unavailable to private litigants, such as threats to terminate public funds for rights violators and the appointment of federal administrators to replace recalcitrant state officials.

The availability and the quality of lawyers also affected the enforcement of civil rights. One reason that early litigation victories had such trivial consequences is that few black lawyers practiced in the South and those who did were often poorly trained. Most white lawyers would not take civil rights cases because of the odium attached to them. The NAACP had limited resources; it was absent from much of the South until the 1940s; and it could not intervene without the assistance of local counsel. After World War II, however, white lawyers were more willing to take civil rights cases and more well-trained black lawyers practiced in the South.

The existence of an organization such as the NAACP proved critical to the effective implementation of civil rights. Isolated Court victories made essentially no difference, as follow-up litigation was invariably required to implement rights. In the absence of a robust NAACP, such litigation proved impossible to sustain. Individual blacks could rarely afford the thousands of dollars necessary to litigate cases through the appeals process. Nor did individuals have much incentive to sue, as litigation generally dragged on for years, disrupting the lives of litigants, while subjecting them to devastating economic reprisals and, occasionally, physical violence.

Only the NAACP, which represented blacks across generations, could capture the benefits of litigation, while spreading the risks and the costs. Without the vast expansion of the association during World War II, the dramatic increases in black voter registration after *Smith* and the widespread assaults on school segregation after *Brown* would not have been possible. Yet the NAACP's virtual monopolization of civil rights litigation was a mixed blessing because it gave white southerners an easy target to attack. Their withering assault on the NAACP in the mid-1950s nearly put it out of business in the Deep South and impeded desegregation litigation.

The relative clarity of legal commands also influenced the implementation of civil rights. Even though most southern federal judges thought that *Brown* was wrongheaded, their sense of professional obligation generally deterred them from defying it; they acknowledged that formal state-mandated school segregation had to end. Yet *Brown II* was so vague as to be meaningless. It provided southern judges with no political cover, which made it difficult for them to aggressively implement it even if they were inclined to do so, which few of them were. Instead, most judges countenanced delay and evasion.

Court decisions are not self-enforcing. Even when civil rights litigants won, their victories meant little unless they possessed sufficient power to enforce them. When southern blacks were most oppressed, they could not even bring equalization suits to challenge the enormous—and obviously unconstitutional—racial disparities that existed in education funding. Challenges to legal lynching reached the Supreme Court only in the 1920s and 1930s, when racial conditions in the South had ameliorated enough to enable civil rights organizations to support such cases. Not a single school desegregation suit was brought in Mississippi until nine years after *Brown*.

Litigation requires lawyers, economic resources, and some security from physical danger. For much of American history, those most in need of racial justice from the courts were least likely to get it, because conditions were too oppressive to permit legal challenges.

Court decisions can also have indirect consequences, such as raising the salience of an issue and energizing the victors (or their adversaries). *Brown* indisputably focused attention on school segregation. People were forced to take a position on the issue, which they had previously been able to avoid doing. For northern liberals in 1954, this inevitably meant opposing segregation. For southern politicians intent on keeping their jobs, however, the only realistic option was to defend segregation and condemn *Brown*.

Brown also inspired blacks to hope and believe that fundamental racial change was possible. *Brown* prompted southern blacks to file petitions and lawsuits seeking school desegregation, shifting their focus away from other issues that had been salient before the Court's ruling—voting rights, school equalization, police brutality, and employment discrimination. This agenda-setting effect of *Brown* was important because southern whites were much more resistant to school desegregation than to many of the other reforms sought by blacks.

There is little evidence that *Brown* educated white Americans to change their positions on school segregation. White southerners bitterly denounced the decision. Most white northerners supported it, but more because they already agreed with its principles than because they were educated by the ruling. Moreover, in the mid-1950s, their endorsement was fairly tepid. Few white northerners supported aggressive enforcement of *Brown* until the early 1960s. Northern opinion on race was educated far more by the civil rights movement than by *Brown*.

Indeed, several of the Court's landmark rulings on race seem to have generated political backlashes rather than educating opinion to support the results. *Prigg v. Pennsylvania* (1842) seemed to inspire northern states to defy the Court by enacting more aggressive measures to protect their free black citizens from kidnapping. *Dred Scott v. Sandford* (1857), which essentially declared the Republican Party unconstitutional by forbidding federal regulation of slavery in national territories, induced Republicans to denounce the Court and rally opposition to it. *Brown* inspired southern whites to mobilize extraordinary resistance to racial change and encouraged extremist politicians to use incendiary rhetoric that fomented violence.

Yet backlashes can produce counterbacklashes, as *Brown* did. The violence that *Brown* induced, especially when directed at peaceful protestors and broadcast on national television, transformed northern opinion on race and paved the way for landmark civil rights legislation.

Civil rights litigation, whether successful or not, served valuable educational, motivational, and organizational functions. NAACP lawyers instructed blacks about their constitutional rights and instilled hope that racial conditions were malleable. Many branches formed around litigation, which also proved to be an excellent fund-raising tool. Black lawyers served as role models to black audiences in courtrooms, as they jousted with whites in the only southern forums that permitted racial interactions on a footing of near-equality, and they demonstrated forensic skills that belied conventional stereotypes of black inferiority.

Before World War II, alternative forms of protest—political mobilization, economic boycotts, street demonstrations, and physical resistance—were largely unavailable to southern blacks, who lived under a ruthlessly repressive regime of Jim Crow. At that time, litigation did not compete with alternative protest strategies for scarce resources, and it offered the advantages of not requiring large-scale participation to succeed and of taking place in the relative safety of courthouses.

Yet litigation by itself could make only limited contributions to racial reform, as early civil rights leaders appreciated. In the 1930s Charles Houston warned that "we cannot depend upon judges to fight ... our battles," and he urged that "the social and public factors must be developed at least along with and if possible before the actual litigation commences." By the 1950s, though, litigation had secured such impressive Court victories and the NAACP was riding so high on its success in *Brown* that direct-action protest may have been slighted, even though it had become a viable option by then. Litigation and direct action now competed for scarce resources, and litigation seemed to have the edge in the 1950s, until the nullification of *Brown* by white southerners demonstrated the limited capacity of lawsuits alone to produce social change.

Though litigation had performed valuable service in mobilizing racial protest and securing Court victories, some of which produced progressive racial change, it could not serve all of the functions of direct action. Sit-ins, freedom rides, and street demonstrations fostered black agency better than did litigation, which encouraged blacks to place faith in elite black lawyers and white judges rather than in themselves. In addition, direct-action protest more reliably created conflict and incited opponents' violence, which ultimately proved critical to transforming national opinion on race.

Charles Hamilton Houston (1895–1950)

"The problem of the Twentieth Century," W. E. B. Du Bois famously proclaimed in 1903, "is the problem of the color line." Du Bois would have been no less accurate had he expanded his claim to cover all of American history.

At the Constitutional Convention in 1787, James Madison repeatedly observed that the principal differences of interest among the states resulted from their varying degrees of dependency on slavery. Seventy-five years later, the nation fought a ghastly civil war over slavery. Conflicting views regarding the rights of blacks were the biggest obstacle to sectional reconciliation in the decades after the Civil War. In the 1960s the nation was riven by civil rights demonstrations, urban race riots, and a militant black power movement. Even today, race is the strongest predictor of national political affiliation.

Tremendous racial progress has been achieved over the course of American history. Slavery and Jim Crow have been abolished. Racially motivated violence has been drastically reduced. Many blacks have made economic, social, and political gains that their grandparents never would have thought possible.

Yet America remains two societies, separate and unequal. *Brown*'s integrationist vision has gone largely unfulfilled. In many spheres, the lives of blacks and whites are more separate than they were fifty years ago. The gains achieved by the civil rights movement have mostly bypassed the black urban underclass. These blacks are poor and getting poorer. They come from broken homes, live in dilapidated and crime-ridden neighborhoods, attend inferior schools, and have few prospects for bettering their lives. No matter how one defines racial equality, it is hard to see how they have achieved it.

Select Bibliography

...

Arsenault, Raymond. *Freedom Riders: 1961 and the Struggle for Racial Justice* (2006).

Ayers, Edward L. *The Promise of the New South: Life after Reconstruction* (1992).

Bartley, Numan V. *The Rise of Massive Resistance: Race and Politics in the South During the 1950s* (1969).

Bartley, Numan V., and Hugh D. Graham. *Southern Politics and the Second Reconstruction* (1975).

Belknap, Michal R. *Federal Law and Southern Order: Racial Violence and Constitutional Conflict in the Post-Brown South* (1987).

Berlin, Ira. *Generations of Captivity: A History of African-American Slaves* (2003).

———. *Slaves Without Masters: The Free Negro in the Antebellum South* (1974).

Boyle, Kevin. *Arc of Justice: A Saga of Race, Civil Rights, and Murder in the Jazz Age* (2004).

Branch, Taylor. *Parting the Waters: America in the King Years, 1954–1963* (1988).

———. *Pillar of Fire: America in the King Years, 1963–1965* (1998).

———. *At Canaan's Edge: America in the King Years, 1965–1968* (2006).

Brauer, Carl M. *John F. Kennedy and the Second Reconstruction* (1977).

Burk, Robert Fredrick. *The Eisenhower Administration and Black Civil Rights* (1984).

Burns, Stewart, ed. *Daybreak of Freedom: The Montgomery Bus Boycott* (1997).

Carson, Clayborne. *In Struggle: SNCC and the Black Awakening of the 1960s* (1981).

Carter, Dan T. *The Politics of Rage: George Wallace, the Origins of the New Conservatism, and the Transformation of American Politics* (1995).

———. *Scottsboro: A Tragedy of the American South* (rev. ed., 1979).

Cecelski, David, and Timothy Tyson, eds. *Democracy Betrayed: The Wilmington Race Riot of 1898 and Its Legacy* (1998).

Chafe, William H. *Civilities and Civil Rights: Greensboro, North Carolina, and the Black Struggle for Freedom* (1980).

Clabaugh, Jason Paul. "Reporting the Rage: An Analysis of Newspaper Coverage of the Freedom Rides of May, 1961," 14 *Southern Historian* 41 (Spring 1993).

Clark, E. Culpepper. *The Schoolhouse Door: Segregation's Last Stand at the University of Alabama* (1993).

Cortner, Richard C. *A Mob Intent on Death: The NAACP and the Arkansas Riot Cases* (1988).

———. *A "Scottsboro" Case in Mississippi: The Supreme Court and* Brown v. Mississippi (1986).

Curriden, Mark, and Leroy Phillips, Jr. *Contempt of Court: The Turn-of-the-Century Lynching that Launched a Hundred Years of Federalism* (1999).

Daniels, Roger. *Asian America: Chinese and Japanese in the United States since 1850* (1988).

Dittmer, John. *Local People: The Struggle for Civil Rights in Mississippi* (1994).

Douglas, Davison M. *Jim Crow Moves North: The Battle over Northern School Segregation, 1865–1954* (2005).

Doyle, William. *An American Insurrection: The Battle of Oxford, Mississippi, 1962* (2001).

Dudziak, Mary. *Cold War Civil Rights: Race and the Image of American Democracy* (2000).

Eskew, Glenn T. *But for Birmingham: The Local and National Movements in the Civil Rights Struggle* (1997).

Fairclough, Adam. *Better Day Coming: Blacks and Equality, 1890–2000* (2001).

———. *Race and Democracy: The Civil Rights Struggle in Louisiana, 1915–1972* (1995).

———. *To Redeem the Soul of America: The Southern Christian Leadership Conference and Martin Luther King, Jr.* (1987).

Farmer, James A. *Lay Bare the Heart: An Autobiography of the Civil Rights Movement* (1985).

Fede, Andrew. *People Without Rights: An Interpretation of the Fundamentals of the Law of Slavery in the U.S. South* (1992).

Fehrenbacher, Don E. *The* Dred Scott *Case: Its Significance in American Law and Politics* (1978).

Finkelman, Paul. *An Imperfect Union: Slavery, Federalism, and Comity* (1981).

———. "The Founders and Slavery: Little Ventured, Little Gained," 13 *Yale Journal of Law and the Humanities* 413 (Summer 2001).

Foner, Eric. *Reconstruction: America's Unfinished Revolution, 1863–1877* (1988).

Fredrickson, George M. *The Black Image in the White Mind: The Debate on Afro-American Character and Destiny, 1817–1914* (1971).

Freehling, Alison. *Drift Toward Dissolution: The Virginia Slavery Debate of 1831–1832* (1982).

Freehling, William W. *The Road to Disunion. Volume I: Secessionists at Bay, 1776–1854* (1990).

———. "Slavery and the Founders," 77 *American Historical Review* 81 (1972).

Freyer, Tony. *The Little Rock Crisis: A Constitutional Interpretation* (1984).

Garrow, David J. *Bearing the Cross: Martin Luther King, Jr., and the Southern Christian Leadership Conference* (1988).

———. *Protest at Selma: Martin Luther King, Jr., and the Voting Rights Act of 1965* (1978).

Genovese, Eugene. *Roll, Jordan, Roll: The World the Slaves Made* (1974).

Gillette, William. *Retreat from Reconstruction: 1869–1879* (1979).

———. *The Right to Vote: Politics and the Passage of the Fifteenth Amendment* (1965).

Gilmore, Glenda Elizabeth. *Gender and Jim Crow: Women and the Politics of White Supremacy in North Carolina, 1896–1920* (1996).

Goodman, James. *Stories of Scottsboro* (1994).

Hacker, Andrew. *Two Nations: Black and White, Separate, Hostile, Unequal* (1992).

Hine, Darlene Clark. *Black Victory: The Rise and Fall of the White Primary in Texas* (1979).

Hirsch, Arnold R. *Making the Second Ghetto: Race and Housing in Chicago, 1940–1960* (1983).

Inger, Morton. *Politics and Reality in an American City: The New Orleans School Crisis of 1960* (1969).

Irons, Peter. *Justice at War: The Story of the Japanese-American Internment Cases* (1983).

Kellogg, Charles Flint. *NAACP: A History of the National Association for the Advancement of Colored People. Volume 1: 1909–1920* (1967).

Klarman, Michael J. *From Jim Crow to Civil Rights: The Supreme Court and the Struggle for Racial Equality* (2004).

Klinkner, Philip A., and Rogers M. Smith. *The Unsteady March: The Rise and Decline of Racial Equality in America* (1999).

Kluger, Richard. *Simple Justice: The History of* Brown v. Board of Education *and Black America's Struggle for Equality* (1976).

Kousser, J. Morgan. *The Shaping of Southern Politics: Suffrage Restriction and the Establishment of the One-Party South, 1880–1910* (1974).

Lane, Ann J. *The Brownsville Affair: National Crisis and Black Reaction* (1971).

Lawson, Steven F. *Black Ballots: Voting Rights in the South, 1944–1969* (1976).

Litwack, Leon F. *Trouble in Mind: Black Southerners in the Age of Jim Crow* (1998).

———. *North of Slavery: The Negro in the Free States, 1790–1860* (1961).

Maltz, Earl M. *Civil Rights, the Constitution and Congress, 1863–1869* (1990).

McAdam, Doug. *Freedom Summer* (1988).

———. *Political Process and the Development of Black Insurgency, 1930–1970* (1982).

McMillen, Neil R. *Dark Journey: Black Mississippians in the Age of Jim Crow* (1989).

———. *The Citizens' Council: Organized Resistance to the Second Reconstruction, 1954–1964* (1971).

McNeil, Genna Rae. *Groundwork: Charles Hamilton Houston and the Struggle for Civil Rights* (1983).

Massey, Douglas S., and Nancy A. Denton. *American Apartheid: Segregation and the Making of the Underclass* (1993).

McClain, Charles J. *In Search of Equality: The Chinese Struggle Against Discrimination in Nineteenth-Century America* (1994).

McPherson, James M. *Battle Cry of Freedom: The Civil War Era* (1988).

Meier, August, and Elliot Rudwick. *Along the Color Line: Explorations in the Black Experience* (1976).

———. *CORE: A Study in the Civil Rights Movement, 1942–1968* (1973).

Morgan, Edmund S. *American Slavery, American Freedom: The Ordeal of Colonial Virginia* (1976).

Morris, Aldon D. *The Origins of the Civil Rights Movement: Black Communities Organizing for Change* (1984).

Morris, Thomas D. *Southern Slavery and the Law, 1619–1860* (1999).

———. *Free Men All: The Personal Liberty Laws of the North, 1780–1861* (1974).

Muse, Benjamin. *Ten Years of Prelude: The Story of Integration since the Supreme Court's 1954 Decision* (1964).

Myrdal, Gunnar. *An American Dilemma: The Negro Problem and Modern Democracy*, 2 vols. (1944).

Nash, Gary B., and Jean R. Soderlund. *Freedom by Degrees: Emancipation in Pennsylvania and Its Aftermath* (1991).

Norrell, Robert J. *Reaping the Whirlwind: The Civil Rights Movement in Tuskegee* (1985).

Nunnelley, William A. *Bull Connor* (1991).

Patterson, James T. Brown v. Board of Education: *A Civil Rights Milestone and Its Troubled Legacy* (2001).

Payne, Charles M. *I've Got the Light of Freedom: The Organizing Tradition and the Mississippi Freedom Struggle* (1995).

Peltason, J. W. *Fifty-Eight Lonely Men: Southern Federal Judges and School Desegregation* (1961).

Perman, Michael. *Struggle for Mastery: Disfranchisement in the South, 1888–1908* (2001).

Robinson, Armstead L., and Patricia Sullivan, eds. *New Directions in Civil Rights Studies* (1991).

Robinson, Donald L., *Slavery in the Structure of American Politics, 1765–1820* (1971).

Schmidt, Benno C., Jr. "Principle and Prejudice: The Supreme Court and Race in the Progressive Era. Part 3: Black Disfranchisement from the KKK to the Grandfather Clause," 82 *Columbia Law Review* 835 (June 1982).

————. "Juries, Jurisdiction, and Race Discrimination: The Lost Promise of *Strauder v. West Virginia*," 61 *Texas Law Review* 1401 (May 1983).

Sherman, Richard B. *The Republican Party and Black America: From McKinley to Hoover, 1896–1933* (1973).

Shoemaker, Don, ed. *"With All Deliberate Speed"; Segregation-Desegregation in Southern Schools* (1957).

Sitkoff, Harvard. *A New Deal for Blacks: Emergence of Civil Rights as a National Issue*. Vol. 1: *The Depression Decade* (1978).

————. *The Struggle for Black Equality, 1954–1992* (rev. ed. 1993).

Smead, Howard. *Blood Justice: The Lynching of Mack Charles Parker* (1986).

Smith, R. C. *They Closed Their Schools: Prince Edward County, Virginia, 1951–1964* (1965).

Steinhorn, Leonard, and Barbara Diggs-Brown. *By the Color of Our Skin: The Illusion of Integration and the Reality of Race* (1999).

Stern, Mark. *Calculating Visions: Kennedy, Johnson, and Civil Rights* (1992).

Sugrue, Thomas J. *The Origins of the Urban Crisis: Race and Inequality in Postwar Detroit* (1996).

Sullivan, Patricia. *Days of Hope: Race and Democracy in the New Deal Era* (1996).

Thornbrough, Emma Lou. *The Negro in Indiana Before 1900: A Study of a Minority* (1957).

————. "The Brownsville Episode and the Negro Vote," 44 *Mississippi Valley Historical Review* 469 (Dec. 1957).

Thornton, J. Mills. *Dividing Lines: Municipal Politics and the Struggle for Civil Rights in Montgomery, Birmingham, and Selma* (2002).

Tindall, George Brown. *South Carolina Negroes, 1877–1900* (1952).

Tushnet, Mark V. *Making Civil Rights Law: Thurgood Marshall and the Supreme Court, 1936–1961* (1994).

————. *The NAACP's Legal Strategy Against Segregated Education, 1925–1950* (1987).

Vorenberg, Michael. *Final Freedom: The Civil War, the Abolition of Slavery, and the Thirteenth Amendment* (2001).

Vose, Clement E. *Caucasians Only: The Supreme Court, the NAACP, and the Restrictive Covenant Cases* (1959).

Ward, Brian, and Tony Badger, eds. *The Making of Martin Luther King and the Civil Rights Movement* (1996).

Weiss, Nancy J. *Farewell to the Party of Lincoln: Black Politics in the Age of FDR* (1983).

———. "The Negro and the New Freedom: Fighting Wilsonian Segregation," 84 *Political Science Quarterly* 61 (Mar. 1969).

Wharton, Vernon Lane. *The Negro in Mississippi: 1865–1890* (1947).

Wiecek, William M. "The Statutory Law of Slavery and Race in the Thirteen Mainland Colonies of British America," 34 (3rd series) *William & Mary Quarterly* 258 (Apr. 1977).

Wilkinson, J. Harvie. *From* Brown *to* Bakke: *The Supreme Court and School Integration, 1954–1978* (1979).

Williamson, Joel. *After Slavery: The Negro in South Carolina During Reconstruction, 1861–1877* (1965).

Woodward, C. Vann. *The Strange Career of Jim Crow* (3rd rev. ed., 1974).

Wright, George C. *Life Behind a Veil: Blacks in Louisville, Kentucky, 1865–1930* (1985).

Wynn, Neil A. *The Afro-American and the Second World War* (rev. ed., 1993).

Young, Jeffrey R. "Eisenhower's Federal Judges and Civil Rights Policy: A Republican 'Southern Strategy' for the 1950s," 78 *Georgia Historical Quarterly* 536 (Fall 1994).

Zilversmit, Arthur. *The First Emancipation: The Abolition of Slavery in the North* (1967).

Index

· · ·